From Abba Dabba to Zorro:
The World of Baseball Nicknames

Don Zminda and STATS, Inc.

Jim Callis and Chuck Miller, Assistant Editors

STATS
PUBLISHING

Published by STATS Publishing

A division of Sports Team Analysis & Tracking Systems, Inc.

This book is dedicated
to James K. Skipper Jr.,
the Babe Ruth
of baseball nickname researchers.

—Don Zminda

Cover by Michael Parapetti

First Edition: May, 1999

ISBN 1-884064-69-8

Acknowledgments

The genesis for *Abba Dabba* began a few years ago when John Dewan, STATS' Chief Executive Officer, suggested that we start compiling nicknames on a systematic basis. From the beginning, it seemed like a great idea. Rob Neyer, who was my chief assistant at the time, enthusiastically took on the task of researching and entering the names, and Rob personally entered most of the thousands of nicknames currently in the database. So I'd like to begin by thanking John and Rob (who currently writes a daily baseball column for espn.com). The foundation for this project really began with them.

When the time finally arrived to craft a book out of that huge database, my staff swung into action. Associate Editor Jim Callis helped manage the details of the project, reviewing every section of the book for clarity and accuracy. Associate Editor Chuck Miller took care of the layout and design; Chuck's clever use of clip-art and photos added greatly to the sense of fun we hope to convey in this book. My chief programmer, Jim Henzler, helped enhance the database so that we could add detailed information on the origin of each nickname. Marc Elman managed the sales and marketing of the book and offered numerous helpful suggestions. Michael Parapetti designed the cover, and part-timers Thom Henninger and Scott King checked stats and helped proofread the manuscript. Thanks also to the other members of my staff: Tony Nistler, Mike Janosi, Mike Sarkis and Antoinette Kelly.

Our recently appointed President, Alan Leib, makes sure that projects like this book help STATS continue to grow. John Dewan and Alan are assisted by Jennifer Manicki. Sue Dewan is in charge of Research & Development/Special Projects.

The Data Collection Department, headed by Doug Abel, gathers all of the unparalleled statistics that are the trademark (literally!) of this company. Doug's staff consists of Jeremy Alpert, Jeff Chernow, Brian Cousins, Ryan Ellis, Mike Hammer, Robert Klein, John Sasman, Jeff Schinski, Matt Senter and Bill Stephens. Together, they oversee our vast reporter network.

The efforts of the Commercial Products, Fantasy, Interactive Products and Sales departments help pay most of our bills at STATS. The Commercial Products division includes Ethan Cooperson, Jim Osborne, David Pinto and Allan Spear. Steve Byrd is in charge of Fantasy, which also consists of Derek Boyle, Dave Carlson, Jim Corelis, Dan Ford, Stefan Kretschmann, Walter Lis, Mark Moeller, Mat Olkin, Oscar Palacios, Corey Roberts, Eric Robin and Jeff Smith. Thanks to Mat, who also helped proof this book. Mike Canter runs Interactive and is assisted by Kevin Fullam, Bart Lilje, Pat Quinn and Nick Stamm. Jim Capuano heads up the Sales team comprised of Scott Enslen and Greg Kirkorsky.

Our Financial/Administrative/Human Resources/Legal Department ensures that everything runs smoothly at our Morton Grove, Ill., headquarters. Howard Lanin and Betty Moy handle the finances. Susan Zamechek oversees the administrative aspects, assisted by Sherlinda Johnson, while Tracy Lickton is in charge of human resources. Carol Savier aids with legal matters. Art Ashley and Dean Peterson provide programming support to all four groups, and Bob Meyerhoff is involved with project management.

Big thanks go to the baseball insiders who contributed nickname lists for the book (along with John Dewan, Rob Neyer and Jim Callis): Dave Anderson, Furman Bisher, Bob Broeg, Gary Carter, John Cerutti, Bob Costas, Ernie Harwell, Tommy Hutton, Tim Kurkjian, Josh Lewin, Denny Matthews, Eric Nadel, Jim Palmer, Ken Singleton, Jayson Stark and Craig Wright. Thanks also to Bill James for contributing the "Notes About Nicknames" chapter.

I mention James K. Skipper Jr., numerous times in the pages of this book. Skipper's incredible book, *Baseball Nicknames: A Dictionary of Origins and Meanings*, is the best source available for anyone who wants to learn about baseball nicknames, and I have gratefully dedicated this book to him.

Thanks, finally, to my family for their patience and support during this project, beginning with my wife Sharon (Honey) Zminda; my dad, Gene (The Old Sidearmer); Sharon's sons Mike (Mookie) and Steve (Cool Breeze) Cacioppo; Mike's wife, Nancy (String Bean) Cacioppo; and that star of the All-Animal team, the wonder dog Ted (Teddy Roosevelt) Cacioppo. Now that's an All-Nickname team!

— Don Zminda (The Zee Man)

Table of Contents

Introduction

What would baseball be like without nicknames?

Well, think about that legendary player. . . you know, George Ruth. The greatest player in the history of the game, a lot of people think. Hit these incredible, long, soaring home runs. Had an incredible flair for the dramatic. And what a character he was. What a zest for living the man had. Good old George.

And Larry Berra. What a smart, wise, funny guy. Just think of some of his pearls of wisdom. "It ain't over 'til it's over." "Nobody goes there because it's always too crowded." "It gets late early there." Larry-isms, they called them.

Or Jay Dean. Old Jay Hanna. What a vivid character *that* guy was. Talked a mile a minute. Won 30 games in 1934, bragging all the way, but nobody hated him for it. Every time I hear the word Jay, it stirs up a thousand memories.

Not quite the same, is it?

Nicknames are part of the lore of baseball, part of what makes the game so vivid. Some players become so linked with their nicknames that the nickname *becomes* their first name, as was the case with Babe Ruth and Yogi Berra and Dizzy Dean. Other nicknames immediately identify a player, like The Splendid Splinter (Ted Williams) or The Yankee Clipper (Joe DiMaggio) or The Man (Stan Musial). Then there are the lesser-known nicknames, ones given to players by friends, family members or teammates. Biscuit Pants for Lou Gehrig. Mex for Keith Hernandez. Bullet for Stu Miller.

We at STATS have been cataloguing baseball nicknames for nearly a decade, entering them into a database that now includes more than 3,000 different monikers. Whenever possible, we log the reason the player got the nickname, the source we first saw it in, and the name of the person who gave the player his nickname. We used this database last year in our massive player encyclopedia, the *STATS All-Time Major League Handbook,* and we've also used it in several other publications. But somehow that didn't seem to be enough. Apart from everything else, nicknames are *fun,* and we decided to try to create a fun book on the subject. The result is the book you're holding in your hands, *From Abba Dabba to Zorro: The World of Baseball Nicknames.*

In this book, we try to look at nicknames from a variety of angles. There's a chapter on the 25 most enduring nicknames in baseball history. There are chapters on players with animal nicknames, players with food nicknames, players with nicknames based on body parts. There's a section on baseball's great nicknamers, one on nicknames of the Negro Leagues, and a chapter listing the best nicknames by position for each major league franchise.

As a bonus, we asked a number of well-known people involved in the game to send us lists of their own favorite nicknames: people like Bob Costas and Jim Palmer and Gary Carter and Ernie Harwell. Each nickname chapter ends with one of the celebrity nickname lists, and we think you'll find them fun and very informative.

We used a number of sources to compile our nickname database, and the primary sources are listed in the Bibliography. But one source stands out above all others: a book entitled *Baseball Nicknames: A Dictionary of Origins and Meanings,* by James K. Skipper Jr. (McFarland & Company, 1992). James Skipper is a sociologist who spent more than a decade researching baseball nicknames, often by directly contacting players, and his book will stand forever as the definitive work on the subject. Our own book is no attempt to compete with Skipper's work, because that simply can't be done. This is meant to be a fun book, a whimsical look at the world of nicknames; his is a scholarly work, a one-volume encyclopedia which thoroughly explores the subject player by player. We credit Mr. Skipper extensively in this book, and we encourage anyone who loves nicknames to explore his superb work.

Don Zminda
Evanston, Illinois
April, 1999

Nicknames A to Z

A is for *Abba Dabba*

Jim Tobin P, 1937-45

Tobin, a knuckleballer who went 105-112 in his nine-year career, used to do a magician's act during which he'd shout, "Abba Dabba, are you ready?" I like to think he shouted the same thing at the hitters as he delivered his knuckler.

B is for *Biscuit Pants*

Lou Gehrig 1B, 1923-39

Not all nicknames are complimentary. Gehrig, a football star during his days at Columbia U., had what Jim Skipper described as a "low center of gravity." I think that means he had a big ass.

C is for *Camera Eye*

Max Bishop 2B, 1924-35

Bishop, the second baseman for the great Philadelphia A's champions of 1929-31, was one of the best leadoff men of his era. In the eight seasons from 1926 to 1933, Bishop drew more than 100 walks seven times. Hence the nickname.

D is for *Dr. Strangeglove*

Dick Stuart 1B, 1958-69

How bad a fielder was Dick Stuart? Bad enough to lead his league in errors by a first baseman in each of his first seven seasons. That includes his rookie year, 1958, when he only got into 64 games at first but still managed to commit a league-leading 16 errors. Stuart's error totals were the kind you'd usually see from a weak-fielding shortstop or third baseman: 29, 24, 22, etc. He was *bad* in the field. . . but he was also colorful, and he could hit.

E is for *Eyechart*

Doug Gwosdz C, 1981-84

```
G
W O
S  D  Z
```

Gwosdz is a lot more famous for his nickname than for his brief 69-game career, spread over four seasons, with the Padres. His name *does* look like a doctor's eye chart, doesn't it? It's pronounced Goosh.

F is for *Flop Ears*

Julie Wera 3B, 1927-29

Along with being the greatest hitter of all time, Babe Ruth was one of baseball's great nicknamers (see p. 23). Ruth never could remember anyone's name, so he often referred to his teammates by their most obvious physical characteristic. Julie Wera became Flop Ears. Myles Thomas was Duck Eye. And Lou Gehrig became Biscuit Pants? That would be a good story, but the Babe usually referred to Larrupin' Lou as Buster.

G is for *Glass Arm Eddie*

Eddie Brown OF, 1920-28

Brown, a pretty good hitter (.303 lifetime) for three National League teams in the 1920s, was reputed to have the weakest arm in the major leagues. If he were playing in the 1990s, he'd probably be a designated hitter with a long career, millions in the bank. . . and no nickname.

H is for *Horse Belly*

Joe Sargent INF, 1921

Joe Sargent's career consisted of only 66 games with the 1921 Tigers, but his nickname will live on forever. So how did a guy who's listed in the record books as 5-foot-10 and 165 pounds wind up with a fat man's nickname? Baseball is full of enduring mysteries.

I is for *Icebox*

Elton Chamberlin P, 1886-96

I don't know much about the caliber of play in the 19th century, but they sure had a lot of great nicknames. Chamberlin, who won 32 games for the 1889 St. Louis Browns, got his moniker as a tribute to his coolness in pressure situations.

J is for *Jughandle Johnny*

Johnny Morrison P, 1920-30

A fine pitcher for the Pirates of the 1920s, Morrison was known for his great curveball, which earned him his moniker. He used it to go 25-13 for the 1923 Bucs, and he also led the National League in saves (not that anyone knew this at the time) in 1929.

K is for *King Carl*

Carl Hubbell P, 1928-43

One of the great pitchers in the period between World Wars I and II, Hubbell pitched the Giants to three pennants in the 1930s. His nickname, given to him by the New York press, was a tribute to his regal pitching. This is a typical sportswriter's nickname—you'd see Hubbell called King Carl in the newspapers, but if you spent some time around the Giant clubhouse, it's doubtful you'd ever hear anyone say, "Hey, King Carl, how ya doin'?"

L is for *Losing Pitcher*

Hugh Mulcahy P, 1935-47

Working for the pathetic Phillie teams of the 1930s and '40s, Mulcahy turned in records like 8-18, 10-20, 9-16 and 13-22 while twice leading the National League in losses. The words "Losing Pitcher—Mulcahy" appeared in so many box scores that they eventually became his nickname. It wasn't really a derogatory term; Mulcahy was an honest workman and a pretty good pitcher who was cursed by a lack of support, and everybody knew it. But it had to grate on him. When World War II began, Mulcahy was the first major leaguer to be inducted into the armed forces. There must have been some comfort in that: For the only time in his career, he found himself working for a winning team.

M is for *Mountain Music*

Cliff Melton P, 1937-44

A country boy from Black Mountain, North Carolina, Melton liked to entertain his teammates by singing and playing the guitar. The lefthander also played some sweet music on the pitching mound, winning 20 games as a rookie for the 1937 Giants. He never pitched quite that well again, but he always had his music to fall back on.

N is for *No Neck*

Walt Williams OF, 1964-75

Walt Williams had no neck! He looked like a cartoon character, like the bad guy had hit him on the head with a mallet over and over until his neck finally disappeared into his body. You had to see him to truly appreciate the effect. Is there a cure for "no-neck disease"? Apparently not, but fortunately the malady wasn't contagious.

O is for *Old Aches and Pains*

Luke Appling SS, 1930-50

From 1930 to 1950, Luke Appling was one of baseball's premier shortstops. The White Sox star won two batting titles, batted .444 in four All-Star games. . . and complained constantly about injuries both real and imagined. He couldn't have been hurt *too* badly, because he was elected to the Hall of Fame in 1964.

P is for *The Pitching Poet*

Ed Kenna P, 1902

The son of a United States Senator, Ed Kenna pitched only briefly in the major leagues: two games (1-1) for the 1902 Philadelphia A's. His main interest was writing poetry, and he eventually left baseball to become a full-time poet. They say his poems were pretty good for the first six or seven stanzas, but then he'd start getting his verses up in the rhyme zone.

Q is for *Quaker*

Johnny Oates C, 1970-81

OK, so it's a little cheap, a little Chris Berman-ish. But how many players have had nicknames that began with Q? Quaker Oates it is.

R is for *Rubberhead*

Cliff Heathcote OF, 1918-32

True story: Cliff Heathcote is playing the outfield for the Cardinals in his rookie season, 1918. He loses a flyball in the sun. Ball bounces off his head. Right away the catcalls begin: "Hey, Rubberhead!" Cursed for life. There, but for the grace of God, goes Jose Canseco.

S is for *Scuzzy*

Ross Grimsley P, 1971-82

Ross Grimsley was a soft-tossing lefthander who went 124-99 for four major league teams, going 20-11 for the 1978 Expos. He was also a pretty weird guy. Grimsley had long stringy hair and a rather sick sense of humor; according to one of his former teammates, Don Baylor, he used to keep a two-foot dildo in his locker. And that was one of his saner habits. So Scuzzy seems about right.

T is for *Twinkletoes*

George Selkirk OF, 1934-42

When the Yankees dumped Babe Ruth after the 1934 season, his replacement was a guy named Twinkletoes. It wasn't pretty. Selkirk, who got his nickname because of his unique running style, was a decent player who went on to have two 100-RBI seasons. But he wasn't Babe Ruth, and the fans and the New York writers never let him forget it. Twinkletoes hung in there, however, eventually becoming the general manager of the expansion Washington Senators of the 1960s.

U is for *Ubbo Ubbo*

Joe Hornung OF, 1879-90

Another great 19th century nickname. Whenever he did something noteworthy on the field, Hornung used to grunt something that sounded like "Ubbo Ubbo." So that became his nickname. Hornung wasn't much of a hitter (.257 lifetime with a pathetic .277 on-base percentage), but he did lead the NL in runs scored in 1883. Ubbo Ubbo!

V is for *Voiceless Tim*

Tim O'Rourke INF, 1890-94

While playing third base for one of his six major league clubs, Tim O'Rourke got hit in

---

the throat by a batted ball. From that point on, his nickname became. . . no, not Rubberthroat, but Voiceless Tim, because the injury rendered him unable to speak for a short time. This never could have happened to No Neck Williams.

W is for *What's the Use?*

Pearce Chiles INF-OF, 1899-1900

Back when I was a struggling young writer still trying to find myself—actually, that seems like me now, except for the "young" part—I was a bit of a pessimist about ever finding success. "Your nickname ought to be 'What's the Use?' " a psychologist once told me. So I really can relate to Pearce Chiles, a dour pessimist whose nickname really *was* What's the Use? Chiles had a great rookie season for the 1899 Phillies, hitting .320 in 338 at-bats. The next year he batted .216, and just like that it was all over. What's the use?

X is for *Double X*

Jimmie Foxx 1B, 1925-45

One of the great sluggers in major league history, Jimmie Foxx got his nickname primarily because of the unique way his last name was spelled. He had another nickname, The Beast, a tribute to his incredible strength and power. But we prefer Double X: the name was a perfect metaphor for the indelible impression that Foxx left on the major league scene.

Y is for *Yo-Yo*

Luis Arroyo P, 1955-63

A lefty screwballer who was one of the first natives of Puerto Rico to make it big in the majors, Arroyo is best known for his fabulous season as the closer for the 1961 Yankees: 15-5 with 29 saves and a 2.19 ERA. He got his nickname during his minor league days, from fans who were having trouble pronouncing his last name.

Z is for *Zorro*

Zoilo Versalles SS, 1959-71

The American League's Most Valuable Player in 1965, Versalles was given his nickname by the Washington Senators' clubhouse attendant early in his career. The name is an obvious variation on Versalles' first name, but it also captures Zoilo's slashing style of play and the way he could rob opposing hitters of base hits.

Bob Costas' Favorite Nicknames

The Wild Horse of the Osage **Pepper Martin**
> "Here's a guy whose name *is* a nickname. Then he gets another *longer* one!"

Double Duty **Ted Radcliffe**

Vinegar Bend **Wilmer Mizell**

The Yankee Clipper **Joe DiMaggio** and
The Splendid Splinter (tie) **Ted Williams**
> "So perfect and so elegant."

The Sultan of Swat **Babe Ruth**

Bob Costas is the voice of Major League Baseball for NBC Sports.

Baseball's 25 Most Enduring Nicknames

To have an enduring nickname, it helps to have an enduring career. Every player on this list is in the Hall of Fame except for two—Joe Jackson and Pete Rose—and it wasn't a lack of career numbers that has kept those two out of the Hall. Of course, not every great player *has* a memorable nickname. I have the video highlights of the 1980 World Series, and the Phillie players keep referring to Mike Schmidt as "Herbie." Sorry, Herbie; you may have been the greatest third baseman in history, but that particular nickname hasn't endured.

So here's my list of the 25 most enduring nicknames in baseball history. You can quibble about some of the names here, but not very much. This is a list of legends of the game, and of players with legendary nicknames.

Hammerin' Hank **Henry Aaron** OF, 1954-76

To be honest, I thought about leaving Aaron off this list; the problem is that another great player, Hank Greenberg, was also known as Hammerin' Hank. But given his accomplishments, I think Aaron will be the Hammerin' Hank we'll remember.

Old Pete **Grover Cleveland Alexander** P, 1911-30

Nobody's really sure how Alexander came to be known as Pete. One story is that he slipped and fell into a pile of peat moss. (In that case, why wasn't the nickname "Old Peat"?) Another story is that during the Depression, booze was referred to as "Sneaky Pete," and Alex definitely liked to imbibe. Whatever; he was Old Pete, and one of the great pitchers of all time.

Yogi **Lawrence Peter Berra** C, 1946-65

The origin of Berra's memorable nickname is something of a mystery as well. Yogi has weighed in on this subject a few times, but to quote the title of one his books, "I Really Didn't Say Everything I Said." We do know that his childhood friends in St. Louis gave him the nickname, and that after his first year or so in the majors, nobody ever referred to him as Larry any more.

The Georgia Peach **Ty Cobb** OF, 1905-28

Well, yes, he was from Georgia, and so are peaches. But no one ever called Ty Cobb a peach of a guy. He probably sliced his peaches open with his spikes, and then spit the pit in your eye.

Dizzy **Jay Hanna Dean** P, 1930-47

Jim Skipper, the brilliant researcher who unearthed the origins of baseball nicknames both famous and obscure (for more on Skipper, consult the Introduction), says that Dean got his nickname during one of his early appearances, an exhibition game against the Chicago White Sox. "Don't let that dizzy rookie fool you," White Sox manager Lena Blackburne shouted to his players. It was the perfect nickname for Dean, one of the most colorful players ever to play the game.

The Yankee Clipper **Joe DiMaggio** OF, 1936-51

"Joltin' Joe" was probably an equally famous nickname for the great Yankee star who died early in 1999. But this nickname conjures up some of the power and majesty which made DiMaggio such a baseball legend. We'll never see the likes of him again.

Rapid Robert **Bob Feller** P, 1936-56

A classic nickname for one of the hardest throwers in major league history. Feller struck out 15 batters in his first major league start at the age of 17, and that was just the beginning. Despite missing nearly four full seasons because of World War II, he still won 266 games.

The Iron Horse **Lou Gehrig** 1B, 1923-39

Gehrig was also known as Biscuit Pants (see p. 4), but in the newspapers he was The Iron Horse (and sometimes Larrupin' Lou). His consecutive-game streak may have been eclipsed by Cal Ripken Jr., but that's done nothing to tarnish his legacy.

Slidin' Billy **Billy Hamilton** OF, 1888-1901

I wanted to put in at least one 19th-century nickname, and this was my selection. It was an ideal nickname for Hamilton, one of the great basestealers of all time.

Rajah **Rogers Hornsby** 2B, 1915-37

Another near-perfect nickname. In reality it's just a variation on the first name of Rogers, but it works because Hornsby was one of the most majestic hitters of all time. Even though he was basically finished as a regular by the age of 33, The Rajah still had 2,930 major league hits.

Shoeless Joe **Joe Jackson** OF, 1908-20

Jackson really did play without shoes in a Carolina Association game in 1908, apparently because his new baseball shoes had given him blisters. He remains one of the game's most tragic figures, banned for life for accepting money to throw the 1919 World Series.

Mr. October **Reggie Jackson** OF, 1967-87

I cover this nickname in more depth in the section on "Great Nicknamin' Teams" (see p. 40). But I couldn't leave Reggie's classic nickname off this list.

The Big Train **Walter Johnson** P, 1907-27

To the overmatched hitters of the 1910s, Johnson's fastball must have indeed looked like a speeding train. In the 15 seasons from 1910-24, Johnson led the AL in strikeouts 12 times, including eight in a row from 1912-19.

Killer **Harmon Killebrew** 1B-3B, 1954-75

In the more politically sensitive era we live in now, I'm not sure a player would be given a nickname like Killer. It's basically a play on Harmon Killebrew's last name, but it fit him very well: the man could kill a baseball.

Matty **Christy Mathewson** P, 1900-16

Mathewson was also known as "Big Six," which was either a reference to his height or to a famed New York fire engine. But to players, fans, and writers, he was always known as "Matty." A true gentlemen and a very intelligent person, Mathewson helped make baseball respectable in the rowdy early days of the 20th century.

The Say Hey Kid **Willie Mays** OF, 1951-73

"Say hey" was one of the young Willie Mays' favorite expressions. He used it so frequently that New York sportswriter Barney Kremenko gave him the nickname The Say Hey Kid. It was even immortalized in a song called "Say Hey (The Willie Mays Song)" by the Treniers. The chorus went:

Say hey (Say who?) Say Willie
Say hey (Say who?) Swingin' at the plate
Say hey (Say who?) Say Willie
That Giant kid is great

Not a bad little song, but Mays had more hits on a good afternoon than the Treniers did in their whole career.

The Little Napoleon **John McGraw** 3B, 1891-1906

John McGraw hated being called Muggsy and would fight anyone who called him by that name. He didn't seem to mind being called The Little Napoleon, a nickname that was a tribute to his skillful managing.

The Man **Stan Musial** OF-1B, 1941-63

Long before every fool in America took to yelling, "You the Man!" Stan Musial—and no one else—was The Man. Musial used to murder Brooklyn Dodger pitching, and some admiring Ebbets Field fans gave him his enduring nickname. He was, without question, one of the half-dozen greatest players in National League history.

Satchel **Leroy Paige** P, 1948-65

The legendary Negro Leagues great got his nickname as a small child when some of his friends saw him carrying several satchels on a long pole. Baseball's notorious color line prevented Paige from reaching the majors until he was 42 years old. But in 1952, the year in which he turned 46, Paige was probably the best relief pitcher in the American League.

Charlie Hustle **Pete Rose** INF-OF, 1963-86

Rose was given his nickname by Yankee great Whitey Ford. Watching Rose run full speed to first base after drawing a walk in an exhibition game, Ford turned to Mickey Mantle and said, "Get a load of Charlie Hustle." I don't think Ford meant it as a compliment, but Rose accepted the nickname proudly. Whatever you may think about his behavior off the field, no one can deny that for 24 years, Pete Rose never stopped hustling.

The Babe **George Herman Ruth** OF-P, 1914-35

There are a number of stories about how Babe Ruth got his famous nickname, but the most credible is that after signing his first professional contract with Jack Dunn's Baltimore Orioles, someone referred to him as "Jack Dunn's babe." He was also known as The Bambino, the Sultan of Swat, Jidge (a variation on George). . . and to many people, the greatest hitter who ever lived.

Baseball's 25 Most Enduring Nicknames   **17**

Duke **Edwin Donald Snider** OF, 1947-64

Snider got his wonderful nickname from his father. When young Edwin walked in from his first day of kindergarten with a proud little bounce in his step, his old man said, "Here comes his majesty, the Duke." Thank you, Mr. Snider. Snider also had a couple of other nicknames, including the wickedly funny California Fruit (see p. 39).

The Flying Dutchman **Honus Wagner** SS, 1897-1917

Question: how did people of German background come to be known as "Dutchmen"? Yeah, I know it stems from Deutschland, but I also know what a Dutchman is, and I'll bet Honus Wagner never wore wooden shoes in his life. What a great player, though. Wagner is still generally regarded as the best shortstop in history, but did you know that he never played 100 games in a season at short until 1903, his seventh in the major leagues? In 1900, the year he won his first National League batting title, Wagner played 118 games in the outfield, nine at third base, seven at second, three at first. . . and none at shortstop. He played shortstop for the first time in the majors in 1901, at the age of 27.

The Splendid Splinter **Ted Williams** OF, 1939-60

You probably could write a book about Ted Williams' nicknames. Or at least a long chapter. When he first came to Boston in 1939, he was known as The Kid. He was also known as The Big Guy, The Thumper, and the nickname Williams gave himself, Teddy Ballgame. (I once had a cat with that name.) The Splendid Splinter was probably his most famous nickname. Even though Williams was splinter-thin for only the first few years of his career, he remained splendid until his last major league at-bat in 1960—a home run, of course.

Yaz **Carl Yastrzemski** OF, 1961-83

When Williams retired after the 1960 season, Carl Yastrzemski took his place as the Red Sox' left fielder. The pressure must have been overwhelming, but Yaz became a hero in his own right, starring for the Sox for 23 years and earning a berth in the Hall of Fame. Yastrzemski's incredible performance in the last days of the epic 1967 American League pennant race remains the stuff of legend. He took the team on his shoulders, carried it into the World Series and finally erased whatever ghosts of Williams still were lingering in the hearts of Sox fans.

Bob Broeg's Favorite Nicknames

The Wild Horse of the Osage **Pepper Martin**

"Pepper Martin fit the Wild Horse nickname pinned on him at Rochester. He played like an untamed mustang."

Goose **Leon Goslin**

"Goslin not only had a surname close to a small goose, a 'gosling,' but his pigeon-toed walk and ample honker were what you would find on your Christmas goose."

The Rajah **Rogers Hornsby**

"With a full handle that made him sound like an orchestra leader, the Rajah had a fancy nickname befitting the king of righthanded hitters."

Dizzy **Jay Hanna Dean**

"The Army sergeant who nicknamed that loosey-goosey, lanky chatterbox on a San Antonio Army base in 1928 'Dizzy' should have been given a medal. As I heard Cardinal manager Gabby Street tell the mayor of St. Louis in 1930, the last day of a pennant-winning season when Diz made his debut a three-hit victory over Pittsburgh, 'Mr. Mayor, I think he's going to be a great pitcher, but I'm afraid we'll never know from one minute to the next what he's going to do!'"

Babe **George Herman Ruth**

"The Babe, by itself and lonesome, still is the most magical name in this century of sports. I don't think 'George' ever could have cut it—even though Foreman is a cuddly character, too."

Bob Broeg's favorite nickname story:

"Perhaps only because I was involved, hearing Brooklyn fans at Ebbets Field intone 'Here comes The Man!', and then having the brain-surgeon mentality to combine The Man with Musial, and, ergo, Stan the Man!"

A St. Louis institution, Bob Broeg has been writing about the Cardinals and baseball for more than 60 years. He was honored with the J.G. Taylor Spink Award by the Baseball Hall of Fame in 1979.

A Few Notes About Nicknames

In *Cobb Would Have Caught It* by Richard Bak, Art Herring, who was called Sandy (which is in the Encyclopedias) reports that this was short for Sandblower, a nickname he was given by Fatty Fothergill. When he asked why he was being called Sandblower, Fothergill explained that it was because he was short, every time he farted he would blow sand in his shoes.

A couple of Royals-related nicknames, one related on the air by Fred White, and the other related on the air by Denny Matthews. Anyway, Fred White, almost verbatim, explaining the trade by which the Royals acquired Yamil Benitez:

"The Royals obtained Yamil in exchange for Mel Bunch, a young righthander from the South. Mel had a wonderful arm, and the day that he reported to spring training, he picked up a nickname that no one ever had to have explained to them.

"(Pause). . . The nickname was Forrest Gump."

The other other story has to do with Galen Cisco, who was the Royals' pitching coach for several years. As Denny Matthews told it, one time Cisco had a boy who was about 14-15 years old who was sitting in a chair down the left-field line, doing ball-boy duty. A screeching one-hopper went down the line, and the Cisco boy made a really nice play on it, so nice that the fans down there applauded.

Well, the next day Matthews saw Galen, and he said, "Hey, nice play your son made there yesterday." Well, Galen's face turned red and the veins on his neck stood out, and he said he had explained to that boy that he wasn't down there to put on no show, and that he was . . and that if he ever did anything like that again, he was going to whale the tar out of him.

And, Mathews added, he wasn't kidding. They didn't call him Grump for nothing.

That's not the *origin* of the nickname, of course. . . that just explains *why* he was called Grump.

The Negro League star, Oliver Marcelle, was called Ghost. Jim Skipper says, as I recall, that he has been unable to locate the source for this nickname. But Buck O'Neill says in his book (*I Was Right On Time*) that they called Ollie Ghost because he would disappear after the game was played; they never saw him between games, didn't know where he was or what he was doing.

— Bill James

Great Nicknamers

1. Charlie Grimm

The happy-go-lucky Cub manager of the 1930s and '40s had a terrific nickname himself, Jolly Cholly. Grimm also had a real gift for giving odd but memorable nicknames to his players. Some examples:

Philabuck **Phil Cavarretta** 1B-OF, 1934-55

When Cavarretta joined the Cubs out of Chicago's Lane Tech high school in 1934, Grimm was serving his first term as the Cubs' manager. He quickly hung this somewhat nonsensical nickname on his young star. What does it mean? Your guess is as good as ours. But it stuck.

Goo Goo **Augie Galan** OF, 1934-49

Galan, who joined the Cubs the same year as Cavarretta, had very large eyes. Goo Goo eyes, apparently, because that became his nickname. Galan used those orbs to good effect, twice leading the National League in walks and compiling a lifetime on-base percentage of .390.

Dim Dom **Dom Dallessandro** OF, 1937-47

Grimm's masterpiece, in my humble opinion. Dallessandro was only 5-foot-6, had an elf-like personality, and crazy things always seemed to be happening to him. The nickname perfectly captured his essence.

Chinski **Charlie Root** P, 1923-41

Another gem from Jolly Cholly. Root, a tough competitor who won 201 major league games, was not averse to pitching inside. Chin music from Chinski, in other words. Root, who served up Babe Ruth's alleged "called shot" home run in the 1932 World Series, claimed that the Babe couldn't have done anything so outrageous. "He didn't point," scoffed Chinski. "If he had, I'd have knocked him on his fanny."

Pruschka **Andy Pafko** OF, 1943-59

When Pafko joined the Cubs during Grimm's second stint as Cub manager, Grimm thought he looked "like he'd just got off the boat from one of those old countries." So Jolly

Cholly gave him an immigrant's name. No doubt Pafko preferred his other (non-Grimm) nickname, Handy Andy.

2. Babe Ruth

As noted in the opening chapter, Ruth had a knack for giving memorable nicknames to other players—mostly because he couldn't remember their real names. The Babe's best:

Flop Ears **Julie Wera** 3B, 1927-29
> See page 5.

Duck Eye **Myles Thomas** P, 1926-30
> According to Jim Skipper, Thomas' eyes were "slightly flattened at the top lids, while the bottoms were generously curved." Just like a duck! At least the Babe thought so.

Broadway **Lyn Lary** SS, 1929-40
> Another Skipper story: when Lary first joined the Yanks in 1929, the Babe asked him where he lived. "Down on Broadway," Lary replied, so that became his nickname. It fit, because like the Babe, Lary liked to party.

Buster **Lou Gehrig** 1B, 1923-39
> You'd think the Babe could remember Lou Gehrig's name, for goodness sake. . . but apparently not. To the Babe, his most famous teammate was some guy named Buster.

3. Tommy Lasorda

Love him or hate him, you have to agree that the Dodgers' long-time manager and executive had a knack for hanging a memorable nickname on a player. A few Lasorda gems:

Wimpy **Tom Paciorek** OF, 1970-87
> When Paciorek first came up to the Dodgers, he went out to dinner with some of the club's more well-heeled prospects like Bobby Valentine, Bill Buckner and Steve Garvey. The bonus babies ordered steaks; Paciorek settled for a couple of double cheeseburgers. Lasorda immediately dubbed him

Wimpy after the hamburger-eating character in the Popeye cartoons.

The Penguin **Ron Cey** 3B, 1971-87

To be honest, Lasorda didn't invent this nickname, which had first been given to Cey during his college years. But Lasorda was the one who made it stick. It's a perfect nickname: With his short legs and low center of gravity, Cey really did look and run like a penguin.

Happy **Burt Hooton** P, 1971-85

This one works because Hooton was anything *but* happy. He seldom smiled and was well known for his sour disposition. You'd think winning 151 major league games would make a guy smile once in a while, wouldn't you?

Bulldog **Orel Hershiser** P, 1983-

When I first heard that Lasorda had christened the tall and skinny Orel Hershiser with the nickname Bulldog, I thought it was a joke. Orel Quinton Hershiser IV. . . Bulldog? But Lasorda had it right; Hershiser *was* a Bulldog, and still is at age 40.

4. Mel Allen

One of the game's first great radio announcers, Allen came up with a number of classic nicknames for the Yankee greats he was describing. Here's a few:

The Yankee Clipper **Joe DiMaggio** OF, 1936-51

Enough said.

Old Reliable **Tommy Henrich** OF, 1937-50

Though not a superstar on the level of a DiMaggio, Henrich was a steady run producer and considered one of the game's best clutch hitters. In his 11-year career, he played on eight pennant winners.

The Plowboy **Tom Morgan** P, 1951-63

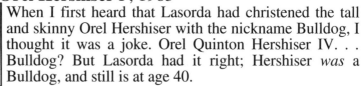

Morgan, a pretty good reliever for the Yanks and several other American League clubs, had a slow, slope-shouldered way of walking in from the bullpen that reminded Allen of a farmer walking behind his plow.

Steady Eddie **Ed Lopat** P, 1944-55

> Simple, but effective. Lopat, a soft-tossing lefty, *was* a very steady performer. He won in double figures in each of his first 11 seasons in the majors, posting a winning record in all but one of those campaigns and recording an ERA over 4.00 only once.

5. Joe Garagiola

Even before he became a Hall of Fame broadcaster, Garagiola was one of baseball's most gifted nicknamers. Some examples:

Cork **Ted Wilks** P, 1944-53

> Wilks was one of the best relief pitchers of the 1940s and early '50s, twice leading the National League in saves. Garagiola, who caught him, called him Cork because of the way he stopped opposing rallies.

Captain Midnight **Lee Walls** OF, 1952-64

> Walls, a teammate of Garagiola's with the Pirates, wore thick aviator glasses. Joe thought they made him look like the goggle-wearing TV character of the early '50s, Captain Midnight.

Mumbles **Bill Tremel** P, 1954-56

> Garagiola also played for the Cubs, where one of his teammates was righty reliever Bill Tremel. The young pitcher was quiet and soft-spoken, and Joe hung this somewhat derogatory nickname on him.

The Big Bear **Fred Hutchinson** P, 1939-53

> Hutchinson became manager of the Cardinals in 1956, around the time that Garagiola joined the St. Louis broadcast team. Joe called Hutchinson The Big Bear because he paced the dugout like a bear on the prowl.

Honorable Mention

Burt Shotton

The long-time major league player, coach and manager only came up with a couple of nicknames, but both were gems: Country, for Enos Slaughter; and Slats, for Marty Marion.

Ken Harrelson

As a player, Harrelson reveled in his own nickname, Hawk. As a broadcaster for the White Sox, he's come up with several enduring nicknames, including Black Jack (Jack McDowell), The Big Hurt (Frank Thomas), The Little Hurt (Craig Grebeck), The Deacon (Warren Newson) and The Little Bulldog (Greg Hibbard). Harrelson may not have invented the nickname One Dog for Lance Johnson; it was given to Johnson, who wore uniform number one, for his ability to track down anything hit to center field. But Harrelson is the one who made it famous, so we'll give him credit for it.

Ken Singleton's Favorite Nicknames

Puddin' Head **Willie Jones**

Rip **Eldon Repulski**

Bullet **Joe Rogan**

Toothpick and *Sad Sam* **Sam Jones**

Stan the Man Unusual **Don Stanhouse**

Ken Singleton on how Dennis Martinez came to be known as El Presidente:

> "Don Stanhouse was unique and got the nickname Stan the Man Unusual from Mike Flanagan. Although Mike gave Stanhouse his nickname, I gave out a nickname that lasted longer than 20 years. Dennis Martinez became El Presidente in 1977 after I hung that moniker on him.

> "When Dennis came to the majors, he arrived with fellow Nicaraguan Tony Chavez. They were the first two players in the majors from that country. So I asked them who was watching the country while they were in the U.S. playing baseball. Soon it was proven that Dennis was the better pitcher of the two, so he became El Presidente and Chavez became Vice Presidente. Dennis stayed in office much, much longer."

Former major league All-Star Ken Singleton is in his third season of broadcasting New York Yankee games for the MSG Network.

Thanks, Dad!

Somewhat less than complimentary nicknames bestowed on players by their fathers, mothers and other family members:

Dodo **George Armstrong** C, 1946

A catcher who got into eight major league games for the 1946 Athletics, Armstrong was given this nickname by his sisters, who didn't think he was very intelligent. I personally would have called him Custer.

Skinny **Hal Brown** P, 1951-64

Another story of warm familial love: Brown was kind of chubby as a child, so his parents called him Skinny. If they wanted him to shape up, he did; Brown slimmed down and went on to have a fine 14-year major league career.

Bozo **Al Cicotte** P, 1957-62

Cicotte, who was the nephew of the famed Black Sox pitcher (and World Series fixer) Eddie Cicotte, liked to eat a kind of ice-cream cone known as a Bozo. His uncle—we're not sure whether it was Uncle Eddie or someone else—noticed this, and Bozo became Cicotte's nickname. We can just hear him saying, "Honest, I was named after an *ice-cream cone!*"

Peanut **Jim Davenport** 3B, 1958-70

Davenport got his nickname from his grandfather, who thought young Jimmy was as small as a peanut. Davenport grew up to be a normal-sized man and a fine third baseman for the San Francisco Giants.

Chubby **Alfred Dean** P-1B, 1936-43

Dean was a little bit chubby at birth, and his older brother gave him the nickname Chubby. It stuck, even though Dean wasn't very portly at all by the time his major league career began in 1936. It was a very unique career; Dean played first base for two years, then shifted to the mound.

Boo **Dave Ferriss** P, 1945-50

Ferriss had trouble pronouncing the word "brother" as a small child. It came out sounding something like Boo, and that became his nickname for the rest of his life. If you're an athlete performing in Boston, you probably don't want a nickname like Boo. Fortunately Ferriss was a good enough pitcher to avoid hearing too many boos. He won 21 games as a rookie in 1945 and 25 more in '46 before hurting his arm. His lifetime record was a splendid 65-30.

Pudge **Carlton Fisk** C, 1969-93

Like Skinny Brown and Chubby Dean, Fisk was somewhat pudgy as a child. So one of his relatives gave him the nickname Pudge. Fisk didn't seem to mind; he lost weight, went on to have a major league career that will probably land him in the Hall of Fame and proudly kept Pudge as his nickname.

Droopy **Chuck Estrada** P, 1960-67

When Estrada was a baby, his father was listening to a radio show which featured a character named Droopy. For some reason Mr. Estrada thought that this was a really cool nickname, so from that point on his young son was known as Droopy. Well, it's better than Bozo, probably. Estrada won 18 games as a rookie for the 1960 Orioles and 15 more in '61. Then his arm started feeling droopy, and he was never the same.

Tookie **Harold Gilbert** 1B, 1950-53

Gilbert, who was the son of famed minor league owner Larry Gilbert, had problems pronouncing the word "cookie" when he was a small child. His brother started calling him Tookie, and the name stuck. Gilbert, who was a minor league slugger, was one of baseball's most highly touted rookies when he came up with the Giants in 1950. But he batted only .203 in his two major league seasons. That's the way the Tookie crumbles, I guess.

Muddy **Harold Ruel** C, 1915-34

When he was a small child, Ruel fell into a puddle and came home soaked and covered in mud. "Look at Muddy over there," said his father, and from that day on, Ruel was known as Muddy. He showed no aversion to dirt in a 19-year career as one of baseball's best catchers.

Squeaky **Fred Valentine** OF, 1959-1968

A switch-hitting outfielder who hit 16 home runs for the 1966 Senators, Valentine was given the nickname Squeaky by one of his aunts. He professed not to know why.

Furman Bisher's Favorite Nicknames

Icebox **Elton Chamberlin**

Old Hoss **Art Twineham**

No Neck **Walt Williams**

The Rabbi of Swat **Mose Solomon**

Shanty **Frank Hogan**

Puddin' Head **Willie Jones**

Atlanta legend Furman Bisher writes about baseball and other sports for the *Atlanta Journal-Constitution*.

Great Nicknamin'
Teams

Some teams seem to be loaded with the sort of vivid personalities that make for good nicknames. And a true sign of camaraderie is a team where the best nicknames aren't just the ones bestowed by friends, family members and sportswriters, but names the players give to each other—often kiddingly, but seldom maliciously. I've chosen three teams from the 1960s and '70s which were particularly good at this. It's probably no coincidence that all of these teams had both a lot of fun in the clubhouse, and a lot of success on the field.

1. Baltimore Orioles, 1960s-'70s

From 1966 to 1979, the Baltimore Orioles were one of baseball's great dynasties, winning five American League pennants. It was a great team overall, and a great team for nicknames. A few examples:

Groove **Don Baylor** OF, 1970-88

The American League MVP in 1979, Baylor had a powerful stroke which produced 338 major league homers. His nickname was a tribute to that sweet swing—he was always in the groove.

Blade **Mark Belanger** SS, 1965-82

An elegant fielder who won eight Gold Gloves at shortstop, Belanger was tall and extremely thin. Just like a blade, his teammates thought.

Toys in the Attic **Frank Bertaina** P, 1964-70

I love this nickname, which I discovered in an old *Sport* magazine article. Though not much of a contributor to the Baltimore dynasty (his lifetime record was 19-29), Bertaina was very intelligent but also more than a little eccentric. The players called him Toys in the Attic after a popular movie of the period.

Motormouth **Paul Blair** OF, 1964-80

Like Mark Belanger, Blair was a defensive wizard who won eight Gold Gloves in center field. He was also the kind of person who never could stop talking, and that was the origin of his nickname.

Clank **Curt Blefary** OF, 1965-72
The AL Rookie of the Year in 1965, Curt Blefary was definitely *not* a defensive wizard; he was strictly in the lineup for his bat. His teammates called him Clank because they thought he had an iron glove.

Crazy Horse **Mike Cuellar** P, 1959-77
A four-time 20-game winner for the O's, Cuellar was extremely superstitious. According to researcher David Petreman, Cuellar believed that his O's cap was blessed by a special spirit, and that he needed to wear it in order to win. His teammates thought this was a little bit crazy, but they couldn't complain about the results.

The Snakeman **Moe Drabowsky** P, 1956-72
One of the real characters of the game, Drabowsky liked to play tricks on his teammates using snakes. Usually they were harmless little grass snakes, but Jim Skipper reports that Moe once left a boa constrictor in Paul Blair's locker, and on another occasion left a four-foot king snake curled up in a basket of dinner rolls. What a guy.

Turkey **Dick Hall** P, 1955-71
A fine reliever for the O's for many years, Hall got his nickname because of his odd delivery; he looked like a turkey flapping its wings. The 6-foot-6 pitcher had another nickname which was given to him while he was pitching in the Mexican winter league: the fans called him Siete Legues (seven Spanish leagues, or roughly thirty acres). I think this means he took up a lot of space.

Chinese **Charlie Lau** C, 1956-67
A reserve catcher who would go on to become a legendary hitting coach, Lau got his nickname because his teammates thought his name sounded Chinese.

Cakes **Jim Palmer** P, 1965-84
There are two stories about how the O's Hall of Fame pitcher got this nickname. Skipper reports that it was a reference to the beefcake poses he made for his legendary Jockey underwear ads. Another story is that Palmer always insisted on eating pancakes on the days he pitched. I personally believe the pancake story is more credible, because I seem to recall Palmer being called Cakes years before he started doing the Jockey ads. But I'm not absolutely sure about that, so I'm reporting both stories.

The Head **Brooks Robinson** 3B, 1955-77

Locker-room humor: the O's Hall of Fame third baseman got this nickname because he was prematurely bald. Robinson had another, somewhat more famous nickname, but I doubt that anyone on the O's bench ever shouted, "Hey, Human Vacuum Cleaner, pass me the pine-tar rag."

The Judge **Frank Robinson** OF, 1956-76

The O's other Hall of Fame Robinson got his nickname because he used to preside over the kangaroo court that the players would hold in the clubhouse. Robinson would dish out insults and two-dollar fines for mental gaffes like throwing to the wrong base or missing a sign. It kept the team focused on the fundamentals, and many other clubs copied the idea.

Stan the Man Unusual and *Fullpack*
Don Stanhouse P, 1972-82

Stanhouse's teammate Mike Flanagan gave him the wonderful nickname Stan the Man Unusual. Stanhouse had an eccentric personality and was maddening to watch on the mound: he had a habit of walking two or three batters before pitching his way out of the jam. It drove manager Earl Weaver crazy; Weaver called him Fullpack because he claimed he would go through a full pack of cigarettes while nervously watching Stanhouse work.

2. Los Angeles Dodgers, 1960s

In their Brooklyn days, the Dodgers were full of colorful characters and great nicknames: Uncle Robbie (manager Wilbert Robinson), The People's Cherce (Dixie Walker) and The Little Colonel (Pee Wee Reese), to name just a few. When they moved to Los Angeles in 1958, they remained both successful and colorful. . . with a bit more of a Hollywood bent. Here's a few of the better nicknames from the Dodgers' glory days of the 1960s:

Possum **Larry Burright** 2B, 1962-64

Burright, an infielder known more for his glove than his bat (.205 lifetime average), was always smiling but seldom had much to say. Teammate Tim Harkness gave him the nickname Possum.

Airdale **Don Drysdale** P, 1956-69

Also known as Big D, the Hall of Famer righthander was given this nickname by teammates Carl Furillo and Joe Pignatano. It's simply a play on Drysdale's last name.

Skoonj **Carl Furillo** OF, 1946-60

Furillo played only briefly in the 1960s, but Skoonj is such a great nickname that I had to include it. It's short for *scungelli*, the Italian word for snail. One story is that Furillo loved to eat *scungelli*; the other is that he was as slow as a snail on the basepaths. I prefer the slow-as-a-snail story, but don't get me wrong: the man could play. Furillo won the NL batting title in 1953, and his throwing arm was regarded as one of the best ever from right field.

The Horse **Frank Howard** OF, 1958-73 and *The Flea* **Bob Lillis** INF, 1958-67

Call this one "The Great Nickname War." Frank Howard was a huge outfielder, 6-foot-7 and about 260 pounds in his Dodger days. Bob Lillis was a 160-pound infielder who hit a total of three home runs in his 10-year career. One day Lillis walked up to Howard in the Dodger clubhouse and said, "You're so big, they oughta call you The Horse!" Howard took offense to this, picked up Lillis by his uniform lapels and screamed, "Oh, yeah? Well, they oughta call *you* The Flea because you're nothin' but a flea on a horse's back!" I'm sure they made up quickly enough, if Howard was even mad. The funny thing was, Lillis' nickname for Howard, The Horse, never caught on (most people referred to him as Hondo), while Howard's nickname for Lillis, The Flea, made in self-defense as much as anything, stayed with Lillis for the rest of his career. Baseball is a funny game.

Frenchy **Jim LeFebvre** 2B, 1965-72

The National League Rookie of the Year in 1965, Le-Febvre's best major league seasons were his first two—years in which the Dodgers won the NL pennant. After that he wasn't much, and his major league career was over at age 30. After spending a few years in Japan, LeFebvre became a manager and piloted the Mariners and Cubs. His nickname stems from his French ancestry.

Pee Wee **Nate Oliver** 2B, 1963-69

In Brooklyn, the Dodgers had a great middle infielder named Pee Wee. Then they moved to LA. Hoping that lightning would strike twice, they tried making Nate (Pee Wee) Oliver their second baseman in 1963. Just like Pee Wee Reese, Oliver was 5-foot-10 and weighed 160 pounds, and of course they shared that great nickname. But that's where the resemblance ended. Oliver did fashion a seven-year career as a utility infielder, but his lifetime average was only .226.

Kemo **Phil Ortega** P, 1960-69

An Arizona native who was a member of the Pima Indian tribe, Ortega's nickname was short for "Kemo Sabe," the term that Tonto used to refer to the Lone Ranger in the 1950s television series. I suppose this was progress of a sort. . . 10 years earlier, Ortega probably would have been known as Chief. Ortega was one of several young starters whom the Dodgers hoped would join Sandy Koufax and Don Drysdale in their powerful starting rotation, but eventually they gave up on him and traded him to the Senators in the deal for Claude Osteen. Ortega had a few decent years for a bad Washington club, winning 34 games from 1965-67.

The Point **Johnny Podres** P, 1953-69

A long-time Dodger starter and the hero of the only World Series the club ever won in Brooklyn, Podres had thinning hair and a somewhat pointy head. So his teammates called him The Point. The lefthander pitched for 15 years in the majors before becoming a successful pitching coach.

The Vulture **Phil Regan** P, 1960-72

After several years as a starting pitcher for the Tigers, Regan came to the Dodgers in 1966 and was shifted to the bullpen. He was an immediate sensation, leading the league with 21 saves and posting a 14-1 record. At least a few of the 14 wins came after Regan had blown a save for Koufax, Drysdale or one of the club's other starters. Other times the starter would leave the game with the score tied, and the club would immediately rally and win the game for Regan. Koufax finally nicknamed Regan The Vulture, saying that Regan was picking the bones of the starting rotation to swoop up victories.

California Fruit **Duke Snider** OF, 1947-64

I'll bet you thought Snider's only nicknames were the Duke, and—later in his career—The Silver Fox. California Fruit was a nickname given Snider by some of his LA teammates, and not a very kind one at that. Long-time teammate Carl Furillo told author Nathan Salant that Snider was always whining about one thing or another, and that even Snider admitted that he was something of a spoiled mama's boy. "California Fruit, we used to call him," said Skoonj. Of course, even Furillo would have to admit that the mama's boy helped the Dodgers cash a lot of World Series checks.

Gropo **Stan Williams** P, 1958-72

Williams was a big, strong guy, and some of his minor league teammates thought he resembled Walt Dropo, a player of similar size. So they called him Gropo. Like Johnny Podres and Phil Regan, Williams had a long, successful major league career, then went on to become a successful pitching coach.

3. New York Yankees, 1970s

What a memorable—and successful—team this was. George Steinbrenner. Billy Martin, in and out. Reggie Jackson. Ron Guidry. Thurman Munson. Goose Gossage. World championships in 1977 and 1978. And some great nicknames, too. Here are a few:

Goose **Rich Gossage** P, 1972-94

One of the greatest relief pitchers of all time, Gossage pitched for 22 years and won three saves crowns. His nickname is a play on his last name, and reminiscent of Hall of Famer Goose Goslin.

Louisiana Lightning **Ron Guidry** P, 1975-88

I'm certain no one called Ron Guidry "Louisiana Lightning" to his face, but it's a great nickname nonetheless. The Louisiana native threw amazingly hard for someone who only weighed 161 pounds, and his Cy Young Award season of 1978 ranks as one of the great seasons in modern times for a starting pitcher (25-3, 1.74).

Catfish **Jim Hunter** P, 1965-79

When Charlie Finley was signing the players who would form the Oakland Athletic dynasty of the 1970s, he wanted them to have colorful nicknames. So he made up the story that Jim Hunter had been given the nickname Catfish as a child after running away from home and returning with two catfish. The story was totally fictitious, but the name Catfish stuck with Hunter throughout his Hall of Fame career.

Mr. October **Reggie Jackson** OF, 1967-87

According to Jackson, the nickname Mr. October was given him by teammate Thurman Munson. That's interesting if true, because it's well known that there was a lot of animosity between Jackson and Munson when Reggie first joined the Yankees in 1977. The nickname is a tribute to Jackson's World Series heroics. But in the League Championship Series, where the pressure is considered even more intense, Jackson was a dud, going .227-6-20 in 45 games. Maybe they should have called him Mr. *Late* October.

Heathcliff **Cliff Johnson** C-1B, 1972-86

A superb bench player who still holds the record for most pinch-hit home runs in a career (20), Johnson was a big, hulking man with an intimidating presence. Skipper says that the name stems from the protagonist Heathcliff in Emily Brontë's *Wuthering Heights*, but you have to ask yourself how many ballplayers have read Emily Brontë. More than likely, the name is simply a play on Johnson's first name.

Count **Sparky Lyle** P, 1967-82

The Yankees' relief ace until Gossage joined the club in 1978, Lyle won the AL Cy Young Award in 1977. Count was short for Count Dracula; Lyle could suck the life out of an opponent's rally like a vampire.

Dude **Rudy May** P, 1965-83

I can never hear the name Dude without thinking of "The Big Lebowski," a movie in which Jeff Bridges played a wacky character known as The Dude. Rudy May was a dude in the same sense that Bridges' character was: both were basically slobs, but colorful characters nonetheless. The well-traveled May pitched in the majors for 16 years, serving two stints of duty with the Yankees.

Stick **Gene Michael** SS, 1966-75

Michael got his nickname because he was tall and extremely thin, like a stick. A light-hitting shortstop, Michael played for the Yanks in the early '70s and later served the club as both its manager and general manager.

Puff **Graig Nettles** 3B, 1967-88

One of great third basemen of all time (390 homers, two Gold Gloves), Nettles was a master needler with a sly sense of humor. He was known for walking up to a group of players, saying something wickedly funny and then disappearing before the victim had a chance to respond. It was like he'd vanished in a puff of smoke, the players used to say.

Sweet Lou **Lou Piniella** OF, 1964-84

Like Gene Michael, Piniella worked for George Steinbrenner as a player, manager and general manager. He could hit a little better than Michael (.291 lifetime), and the nickname Sweet Lou was a tribute to his sweet swing.

Gozzlehead **Mickey Rivers** OF, 1970-84

The center fielder on the Yankees' championship clubs of 1977-78, Rivers was also known as Mick the Quick (he stole as many as 70 bases in a season) and Mickey Mouth (he never stopped talking). As for Gozzlehead, let's just say the name is a tribute to Mickey's unique personality. He could play the game, but sometimes he didn't seem to be all there mentally.

Chicken **Fred Stanley** SS, 1969-82

A backup middle infielder for most of his career, Stanley was very skinny and had an odd way of walking, sort of like a chicken. So the Yanks had both the Stick and the Chicken to handle shortstop. Kind of poetic, don't you think?

Dirt **Dick Tidrow** P, 1972-84

One of the relievers who pioneered the role of setup man, Tidrow was given the nickname Dirt by one of the pitchers he set up, Sparky Lyle. The Yankees used to play a pepper game called flip prior to the ballgame, and Tidrow would always be diving into the dirt and getting his uniform filthy in order to grab the ball.

Style Master **Jeff Torborg** C, 1964-73

Torborg became a Yankee coach in the late 1970s, but prior to that he managed the Indians for a couple of years. The Yankee players used to make fun of the way Torborg would walk slowly out to the mound to change pitchers, his uniform starched and unwrinkled and his cap set perfectly on his head. Graig Nettles gave him the nickname Style Master, as in "Hey, Style Master, you have a hair out of place!" I wonder if they still called him that after he joined the Yanks.

Honorable Mention

St. Louis Cardinals, 1934

The Gashouse Gang won only one pennant, but it remains one of the legendary teams in baseball history. And what terrific nicknames: Dizzy and Daffy (the Dean brothers), The Lip (Leo Durocher), Ducky Wucky (Joe Medwick), Wild Bill (Bill Hallahan), Ripper (Jim Collins).

New York Yankees, 1930s-'40s

Along with a great club on the field, the Bronx Bombers of the post-Babe Ruth era had some memorable nicknames: The Iron Horse (Lou Gehrig), The Yankee Clipper (Joe DiMaggio), Old Reliable (Tommy Henrich), Twinkletoes (George Selkirk), Flash (Joe Gordon), Goofy (Lefty Gomez).

St. Louis Cardinals, 1940s

The Cardinal champions of the 1940s boasted The Man (Stan Musial), Country (Enos Slaughter), Slats (Marty Marion), The Hat (Harry Walker), Hippity (Johnny Hopp), The Arkansas Hummingbird (Lon Warneke), Four Sack (Erv Dusak) and Cork (Ted Wilks).

Jim Palmer's Favorite Nicknames

Wacko **Rich Dauer**

Turkey **Dick Hall**

Bullet **Stu Miller**

Tired **Eddie Murray**

Samurai Second Baseman **Lenn Sakata**

Crazy Horse **Mike Cuellar**

Jim Palmer on why Mike Cuellar was known as Crazy Horse:

> "Cuellar hits a triple in Tiger Stadium. He ignores Cal Ripken Sr.'s stop sign and just keeps running. The ball gets away and he scores. He could really pitch, but baserunning was a different story."

Hall of Famer Jim Palmer broadcasts Oriole games for Home Team Sports.

That's Showbiz

Players named after characters of the stage, screen, radio and television:

The Swamp Fox **Marshall Bridges** P, 1959-65

A colorful lefty reliever who was immortalized in Jim Brosnan's *Pennant Race*, Bridges came from the swamp country of Mississippi. He was named after the main character in the Disney series "Swamp Fox," which chronicled the adventures of Revolutionary War hero Francis Marion.

Mr. Chips **Bob Chipman** P, 1941-52

"Goodbye Mr. Chips" was an Academy Award-winning film in 1939 starring Robert Donat. When lefthanded pitcher Bob Chipman joined the Dodgers two years later, it was no surprise that he was given the nickname Mr. Chips. Chipman turned out to be a pretty good pitcher, and didn't say goodbye to the major league scene for 12 years.

Rambo **Mike Diaz** 1B-OF, 1983-88

Diaz was a big, strong guy who bulked himself up like Sylvester Stallone in the "Rambo" movies. It paid off; in his brief four-year career, Diaz belted 31 homers in only 683 at-bats. The only mystery is why he wasn't given more of a chance to play.

Gomer **Harold Hodge** INF, 1971

Hodge came from North Carolina, and his teammates thought he sounded like Jim Nabors in the "Gomer Pyle" television series. Hodge spent one year in the majors as a pinch-hitting specialist for the Indians. When he batted only .205, Gomer was a goner. Shazam!

Buster **Rickey Keeton** P, 1980-81

Keeton was named after Buster Keaton, the great silent film star of the 1920s. He couldn't silence the opponents' bats, so he was gone after two years.

King Kong **Charlie Keller** OF, 1939-52

According to Jim Skipper, Keller was considered the strongest player of his era. King Kong was reputed to be the strongest gorilla. A terrific hitter, Keller might have had a Hall of Fame career if not for a serious back injury.

Spanky **Ed Kirkpatrick** C-OF, 1962-77

Kirkpatrick was a bit pudgy and disheveled, and a Kansas City Royals fan thought he looked like Spanky McFarland in the "Our Gang" movie shorts. Spanky could spank the ball a little, and though he seldom played regularly, he lasted in the majors for 16 years.

Cab **Don Kolloway** INF, 1940-53

Kolloway was named after Cab Calloway, the famed night-club performer. Kolloway never sang "Minnie the Moocher," but he did play against Minnie Minoso—and a lot of other great players—during his 12-year American League career.

Fibber **Bill McGhee** 1B, 1944-45

"Fibber McGee and Molly" was one of the most popular radio shows of the 1930s and '40s, and any player named McGee or McGhee was apt to wind up with the nickname Fibber. This McGhee was an underpowered first baseman who played for the A's during World War II.

Tarzan **Roy Parmelee** P, 1929-39

Parmelee got his nickname not because of his physical strength, but because—as one New York writer put it—"his work on the mound usually leaves him out on a limb." Parmelee was a hard-throwing righthander, but he didn't always know where his pitches were going. He led the National League in walks once, in wild pitches twice and in hit batsmen three times. His wildness retarded his progress, and he never won more than 14 games in a season.

Lurch **Steve Renko** P, 1969-83

Renko was a big, strong guy, 6-foot-5 and 230 pounds, with a hulking presence. He reminded people of Lurch, the 7-foot butler played by Ted Cassidy in "The Addams Family" television series. Despite his appearance Renko was an excellent athlete who'd been the starting quarterback at the University of Kansas, playing in the same backfield with Gale Sayers. He pitched in the majors for 15 years and won 134 major league games.

Charley Chan **Charley Schanz** P, 1944-50

The Charlie Chan movies were a staple of the 1940s, and when the Phillies brought up a pitcher named Charley Schanz in 1944, you knew what his nickname was going to be. Schanz had a nice rookie year, winning 13 games for a last-place ballclub, but he won only 15 more games in his career.

Sabu **Bill Schuster** INF, 1937-45

Schuster had an awful lot of notoriety for a player who batted only 261 times in the majors with a .234 average. He was known for loving the bright lights, and one of his nicknames was Broadway. The nickname Sabu came from the loud yells which Schuster used to let loose with during games. It reminded people of the elephant calls made by Sabu the Elephant Boy in a series of movies which were popular at the time.

Joe E. **Thurman Tucker** OF, 1942-51

White Sox and Indian outfielder Thurman Tucker wore glasses and had a face that looked like a horse. He was pretty much a dead ringer for the movie comedy star Joe E. Brown, a big baseball fan whose son Joe L. went on to become general manager of the Pirates. I've seen pictures of Tucker standing next to the original Joe E., and it's hard to tell them apart. Tucker wasn't much of a hitter (.255 lifetime), but he was an excellent outfielder who led AL flychasers in putouts in 1943.

Tarzan **Joe Wallis** OF, 1975-79

We've already done one Tarzan, but Joe (Tarzan) Wallis deserves mention, also. A fan favorite, Wallis got his nickname because he used to like diving out of hotel windows into swimming pools. The bleacher crowds at Wrigley loved him, but he never hit enough to win a regular job (.244 lifetime).

John Cerutti's Favorite Nicknames

Terminator **Tom Henke**
"I gave Tom Henke his nickname in 1985 while we were roommates playing Triple-A with Syracuse. We were in Richmond and watched 'The Terminator' in our hotel room one night. The next day at the park, while Tom lumbered down to the bullpen, he reminded me of Arnold Schwarzenegger in the movie. I called him Terminator. It stuck. Of course, at the time he was on a streak of 33 consecutive scoreless innings."

Cy Weed **Dave Stieb**

Gadget Man **Tony Fernandez**

Razor **Rance Mulliniks**

Pee Wee **Jimmy Key**

Cuffs **Bill Caudill**

Bone **Rick Leach**

Former Toronto pitcher John Cerutti broadcasts Blue Jay games for CTV.

The Players' Restaurant

The All-Food Team

MGR	*Cookie*	Harry Lavagetto, 1957-61
C	*Cracker*	Ray Schalk, 1912-29
1B	*Big Mac*	Mark McGwire, 1986-
2B	*Spinach*	Oscar Melillo, 1926-37
3B	*Pie*	Harold Traynor, 1920-37
SS	*The Tabasco Kid*	Norman Elberfeld, 1898-1915
LF	*Goose*	Leon Goslin, 1921-38
CF	*Turkey Mike*	Mike Donlin, 1899-1914
RF	*Chili*	Charles Davis, 1981-
SP	*Stew*	Dave Stewart, 1978-95
RP	*Huevo*	Vicente Romo, 1968-82
UTIL	*Suds*	Bill Sudakis, 1968-75

And now, our menu:

Breakfast

Juice **Julio Cruz** 2B, 1977-86

The second baseman on the White Sox' American League West champions of 1983, Cruz wasn't much of a hitter (.237 lifetime), but he had a good glove and great speed, stealing 40-plus bases for seven straight seasons (1978-84). Juice was a play on his first name, one of the many nicknames popularized (if not invented) by Sox announcer Hawk Harrelson.

Grapefruit **Jim Yeargin** P, 1922-24

Jim Skipper says he doesn't know the origin of Jim Yeargin's nickname, so let me try: he lobbed the ball to the hitters like a grapefruit and said, "Hit it, boys." Which they did. Yeargin's lifetime record was 1-12.

Bananas **Zeke Bonura** 1B, 1934-40

Bonura got his primary nickname, Zeke, because he had a muscular physique. He got the nicknames Bananas and Banana Nose because of his super-sized nose. Bonura could hit—his lifetime average was .307 and he had four 100-RBI seasons—but he was regarded as such a weak fielder at first base that his half-hearted waves at balls hit a step or two to his right became known as "Bonura salutes."

Prunes **George Moolic** C, 1886

Another cool nickname with an origin that is still a mystery. I don't know how Moolic got it, either, but I do know that he had great difficulty producing runs. He batted .143 in his only major league season.

Eggie **Ed Lennox** 3B, 1906-15

What would breakfast be without eggs? This one is pretty simple to explain: Eggie is just a variation on Edgar, Lennox' first name. Eggie wasn't a star, but he could bring home the bacon on occasion. He batted .274 with good peripheral stats in a light-hitting era.

Huevo **Vicente Romo** P, 1968-82

Romo got his nickname while still an amateur pitcher in his native Mexico. Huevo is Spanish for egg, and one of his managers thought he had an egg-shaped face. Romo had a decent career as a reliever, pitching for five clubs.

Link **Bobby Lowe** 2B, 1890-1907

A bit of a stretch, perhaps, but you have to have some link sausages with those eggs, don't you? Lowe, who got his nickname because his middle name was Lincoln, is best known as the first player ever to hit four homers in a game. He did it on May 30, 1894, in Boston's South End Grounds, not exactly a tough home-run park. That year Lowe hit a career-high 17 home runs, 16 of them at home.

Bun **Robert Troy** P, 1912

A Sticky Bun, maybe? Troy's something of a mystery man. His career consists of one game started for the 1912 Tigers (6.2 innings, four runs), his only major league appearance, and no one knows the origin of his nickname.

Oats **Joe DeMaestri** SS, 1951-61

A slick-fielding shortstop for several American League clubs in the '50s, DeMaestri was also known as Froggy (see p. 123). He got the nickname Oats as a child because of his oatmeal-colored hair. Oats wasn't much of a hitter (.236 lifetime), but his glove kept him employed by major league teams for more than a decade.

Peaches **George Graham** C, 1902-12

Graham supposedly got his nickname because fans considered him "a peach of a catcher." Isn't that peachy? Some people believe that Graham was the same person as Billy Maharg (Graham spelled backwards), one of the fixers of the 1919 World Series. That *wouldn't* be peachy, but most evidence indicates that Graham and Marharg were different people.

Doughnut Bill **Bill Carrick** P, 1898-1902

Carrick was a hard-working, but not very successful, pitcher for the Giants and Senators at the turn of the century. In 1899 he gave up a staggering 485 hits in 361.2 innings, and his career featured records like 16-27, 19-22 and 14-22. Since Carrick got his nickname because of his fondness for doughnuts, this will serve as a cautionary tale on the dangers of failing to eat a nutritious breakfast.

Pound Cake **Chuck Harrison** 1B, 1965-71

Another junk-food junkie. Harrison was short and stocky, and apparently fond of his sweets. No one would have minded had he pounded the ball the way he hit the pound cake, but Harrison was a .238 lifetime hitter who never hit more than nine dingers in a season.

Cocoa **Dan Woodman** P, 1914-15

Woodman spent his entire career in the short-lived Federal League (1914-15). He had good success in his brief career (2.94 ERA in 18 games), but like a lot of the Feds, he didn't get picked up by a major league club after the league folded. The origin of his nickname is unknown.

Coffee Jack **Jack Ryan** P, 1908-11

A spitballer with a brief but successful career (2.88 ERA in 24 games for the Indians and Red Sox), Ryan produced saliva by chewing on slippery elm mixed with coffee grounds. Sounds delicious.

Sugar **Bob Cain** P, 1949-54

There have been several players named Cain or Kane in major league history, and almost all of them have been nicknamed Sugar. This Cain was a lefty who had a couple of 12-win seasons in the early 1950s. He is best known for defeating Bob Feller, 1-0, in a duel of one-hitters in 1952.

Mid-Morning Break

Ding Dong **Gary Bell** P, 1958-69

Time for a little mid-morning pick-me-up. Bell got his nickname not because he was fond of Hostess Ding-Dongs—I believe he was more of a Twinkies man—but as a response to the last name of Bell. He was a pretty good pitcher, winning 121 games in his career.

Candy **William Cummings** P, 1876-77

Cummings is credited with being the first pitcher to perfect the curveball, and he got his nickname because his pitching was a sweet thing to watch. His career was winding down by the time the National League opened for play in 1876, and he won only 21 games in the majors. Nonetheless he was elected to the Hall of Fame in 1939.

Cookie **Octavio Rojas** 2B, 1962-77

A 16-year veteran who could play virtually any-where on the diamond, Rojas was a Cuban whose nickname originally was Cuqui. He had some good years for the Phillies and Royals and later managed the Angels for a season.

Smoke **Joe Kiefer** P, 1920-26

Time for a smoke. Like most players with this nickname, Kiefer received it in recognition of his good fastball. He may have had a good heater, but he didn't have much major league success: he was 0-5 lifetime with a 6.16 ERA.

Matches **Matt Kilroy** P, 1886-98

Well, we need something to light our smoke with, right? An excellent pitcher for Baltimore in the American Association in the late 1880s, Kilroy still holds the all-time record for most strikeouts in a season. He fanned 513 batters in his rookie year, 1886; of course he worked a few more innings (583) than Nolan Ryan did. The heavy workload caught up with him, and he faded out after a few years. Kilroy's nick-name is a corruption of his first name, Matthew.

Toothpick **Sam Jones** P, 1951-64

For those trying to avoid cigarettes, there's always nibbling on a toothpick. Also known as Sad Sam, Jones got his nick-name because of his habit of chewing on a toothpick while on the mound. The hard-throwing righty led the National League in strikeouts three times in the 1950s. He also tossed a memorable no-hitter against the Pirates in 1955 in which he loaded the bases with walks to start the ninth in-ning, then struck out Dick Groat, Roberto Clemente and Frank Thomas.

Lunch

Soup **Clarence Campbell** OF, 1940-41

When your last name is Campbell, it's not surprising that you might be known as Soup. This Campbell was a so-so player (.246) who spent a couple of years with the Indians.

Pea Soup **George Dumont** P, 1915-19

Dumont spent a few years with the Senators and Red Sox and compiled a solid 2.85 ERA, but his lifetime record was 10-23. Unfortunately, no one seems to know why he was known as Pea Soup.

Noodles **Frank Hahn** P, 1899-1906

According to Lee Allen, Hahn used to bring lunch to his father every day when he was a child. The lunch was always the same—noodle soup—so young Hahn became known as Noodles. Though his career was shortened by injuries, Hahn had some terrific years for the Reds, winning 20 games four times and compiling a lifetime ERA of 2.55.

Cracker **Ray Schalk** C, 1912-29

Though not much of a hitter (.253 lifetime), Schalk was such an outstanding catcher that he was elected to the Hall of Fame in 1955. It's said that he recorded a putout at every base during his catching career. No one quite knows how he got his nickname. It's one usually given to players from the South, but Schalk was a native of Harvey, Illinois.

Big Mac **Mark McGwire** 1B, 1986-

A little cheap, I'll admit, but don't the words Big Mac connote "lunch" to most people? Not to mention the fact that McGwire's home runs are "super-sized."

Sub **Eldon Auker** P, 1933-42

Since I'm going to count Big Mac as a food nickname (not to mention Smoke and Matches), why not Sub? A successful pitcher for the Tigers' pennant-winning clubs of the 1930s, Auker threw the ball submarine-style.

Super Sub **Phil Linz** INF, 1962-68

We're on a roll here. Linz got his nickname because he could fill in at several different positions for the Yankees. The most memorable incident of Linz' career happened off the field, after the Yankees had lost a tough series to the White Sox in 1964. With the whole team steaming while the club rode the team bus to the airport, Linz had the audacity to start playing "Mary Had a Little Lamb" on his new harmonica. Rookie manager Yogi Berra got mad and knocked the mouth organ out of Linz' hands, thus asserting his authority for the first time. And the Yankees went on to win the pennant. Who knows. . . had Linz been quietly eating a submarine sandwich instead of playing the harmonica, the Yanks might never have won the pennant.

Chili **Charles Davis** OF, 1981-

Davis got his memorable nickname as a child after getting a particularly ugly haircut. His friends

---

started making fun of the haircut and calling him "Chili Bowl," a name that was later shortened to Chili. Davis must not have minded too much, because he's been Chili Davis ever since.

Stew **Dave Stewart** P, 1978-95

Got to have some stew on our lunch menu, right? Though he took a while to establish himself, Stewart became a fearsome pitcher for Tony La Russa's A's, winning 20 games for four straight years.

Skins **Johnny Jones** OF, 1923-32

Potato skins. . . wow, I'm getting hungry! I don't know the origin of Johnny Jones' nickname, but I do know that he had a very unique career. After getting into one game for the A's in 1923, Jones went back to the minors, where he languished for nine years. Temporarily out of work when the Eastern League folded in 1932, he decided to attend an A's game. As luck would have it, A's outfielder Doc Cramer got hurt early in the game, and Connie Mack was desperate for a replacement; knowing Skins was in the stands, he had him paged and immediately put him into the game (I presume they found a uniform for him). It would be nice to report that Skins did a Roy Hobbs and led the A's to the pennant, but after going 1-for-6, he was sent back down to the minors.

Buttermilk Tommy **Tommy Dowd** OF-2B, 1891-1901

Dowd was a speedy outfielder for the St. Louis Cardinals of the 1890s. He had his best year in 1893, stealing 59 bases and scoring 114 runs. I don't know the origin of his nickname.

Afternoon Snack

Snacks **Ray Shore** P, 1946-49

Ray Shore pitched briefly but unsuccessfully for the Cardinals in the late 1940s, posting an 8.23 ERA. He then went on to a very successful career as a major league scout, working mostly for the Cincinnati Reds. He loved his snacks, and that's how he got his nickname.

Cheese **Al Schweitzer** OF, 1908-11

 Schweitzer's nickname, according to Skipper, is a response to the last name of Schweitzer. He is not to be confused with the great humanitarian of the same name,

Albert Schweitzer. (And don't confuse him with Peaches Graham, either.) Schweitzer had pretty good speed, but his lifetime average in four years with the Browns was only .238.

Slim Jim **Howard Earl** OF-2B, 1890-91

Earl got his nickname not for his fondness for Slim Jims, but because he was very skinny. He had a pretty slim major league career, batting .248 in two seasons in the 1890s.

Cookie **Harry Lavagetto** 3B, 1934-47

Time for another cookie. An Oakland native, Lavagetto signed as a teenager with Cookie DeVincenzi's Oakland Oaks of the Pacific Coast League. DiVincenzi took the Italian youngster under his wing, and Harry became known as Cookie's Boy and later as Cookie. Lavagetto played for 10 years with the Pirates and Dodgers, ending his career in memorable fashion by breaking up Bill Bevens' no-hit bid with two out in the ninth inning of Game 4 of the 1947 World Series. Lavagetto's hit not only broke up the no-hitter, but gave the Dodgers the victory. He later managed the Washington Senators.

Candy Man **John Candelaria** P, 1975-93

Why not some more candy as well? An outstanding lefthander who pitched for 19 years in the majors, Candelaria won 177 major league games. His best season came in 1977, when he went 20-5 with a National League-leading 2.34 ERA for the Pirates.

Lollipop **Wade Killefer** OF-2B, 1907-16

The younger brother of major league catcher Bill Killefer, Wade Killefer played for four major league clubs, filling in all over the diamond. He had bright red hair, bright as a red lollipop, and he also was known as Red.

Taffy **Taft Wright** OF, 1938-49

Wright was a good-hitting outfielder for several American League clubs, hitting .311 lifetime. In 1941, he set an AL record by driving in runs in 13 consecutive games. His nickname is simply a variation on his first name, Taft.

Shakes **Walter Huntzinger** P, 1923-26

No, he wasn't overly fond of chocolate shakes, to my knowledge. Huntzinger got his nickname because when he got a good hand in a poker game, his hands would start shaking. I don't know whether his hands shook on the mound as well, but he wasn't a bad pitcher, recording a 3.60 lifetime ERA.

Apples **Andy Lapihuska** P, 1942-43

Another nickname with origins that are a mystery. Lapihuska was strictly a wartime fill-in for the Phillies, recording a 7.04 ERA in four games. The Phils didn't like them apples, and sent Lapihuska on his way.

Pretzels **John Pezzullo** P, 1935-36

Pretzels is partly a variation on John Pezzullo's last name, partly a reference to the twisting, herky-jerky windup he employed. The delivery didn't fool too many hitters, as his lifetime ERA was 6.36.

Peanuts **Harry Lowrey** OF, 1942-55

Lowrey got his nickname as an infant when his uncle exclaimed, "Why, he's no bigger than a peanut!" Young Peanuts grew up to be a quality major leaguer, hitting .273 lifetime.

Chewing Gum **John O'Brien** 2B, 1891-99

O'Brien got his nickname because he was a gum chewer in an era when most players chewed tobacco. The big sissy. A .254 lifetime hitter, he played for six teams in his six-year career. Now if he had only chewed tobacco like the rest of the guys. . .

Smoke **Dave Stewart** P, 1978-95

Yes, it's time for another smoke, and time for Dave Stewart again. Stewart's lifetime record in postseason play was 10-6, including 8-0 in the LCS.

Cocktail Hour

Sour Mash Jack **Jack Daniels** OF, 1952

When your name is Jack Daniels, can you possibly escape a nickname like this one? Daniels played one season for the Braves, getting in 106 games in 1952. When he batted only .187, the head bartender in the Braves' front office said, "I think you've had enough."

Brandy **Robert Davis** OF, 1952-53

Davis got his nickname from his middle name, Brandon. Like Jack Daniels, he played for a bad National League club in the 1950s (the Pirates), and like Daniels, he batted only .187. The only difference is that he lasted a year longer than Jack did. I guess you gulp down your Jack Daniels, but you sip your Brandy for a little while.

Three Star **George Hennessey** P, 1937-45

Hennessey Three Star is another fine beverage. Unlike Daniels and Davis, Hennessey was a pitcher, but he didn't have much success, either: his lifetime ERA was 5.20. Major league teams sipped this Hennessey very slowly: five games with the Browns in 1937, five with the Phillies in 1942 and two with the Cubs in 1945. By then he was 37 years old: well-aged, I'd say.

Jigger **Arnold Statz** OF, 1919-28

A long-lasting drink at last. Statz played eight years in the majors, hitting a solid .285, but won his greatest fame in the Pacific Coast League. He played 18 seasons for the Los Angeles Angels and compiled an amazing 3,356 hits as a minor leaguer. Between majors and minors, he amassed 4,093 hits. Statz was also an excellent golfer and his nickname Jigger came from the name of a golfer's iron.

Highball **Howard Wilson** P, 1899-1904

The origin of Wilson's nickname isn't clear, but he could be forgiven for putting away a few highballs while thinking about his rotten pitching luck. Despite a respectable career ERA of 3.29, his lifetime record was 14-27.

Brewery Jack **Jack Taylor** P, 1891-99

There were two Jack Taylors pitching in baseball between 1890 and 1910, both of them pretty talented. The first Jack Taylor was known as Brewery Jack because he liked to imbibe; the second was known as Brakeman Jack because he worked for a railway company in the offseason. Brewery Jack supposedly hit the bottle a little harder than was good for him, but his biggest problem was Bright's Disease, a kidney disorder which began to affect him late in his career. Taylor pitched in only 24 games in 1899, and he died the following February.

Suds **Bill Sudakis** INF, 1968-75

Sudakis was a versatile switch-hitter who could play a number of different positions. He batted only .234 lifetime, but his versatility and home-run power (he hit 15 homers once and had a pair of 14-homer seasons) kept him around for eight major league seasons. Suds is simply a play on his last name.

Dinner

Seafood

Oyster **Tommy Burns** OF-INF, 1884-95

Burns was one of the most versatile players of all time. He could play any outfield and infield position and even pitched when needed, compiling a lifetime record of 8-5. A lifetime .300 hitter, he led the National League in home runs and RBI in 1890. He got his nickname because he loved to eat oysters.

Bass **Les Fleming** 1B, 1939-49

Fleming, a first baseman with decent pop, was known as Bass because he loved bass fishing. In 1942, the only year he played regularly, he had a .292-14-82 season for the Indians while drawing 106 walks.

Snapper **Ford Garrison** OF, 1943-46

Garrison got his nickname not because he liked to eat snapper, but because his father hoped he would become a jockey. He gave his son the nickname Snapper in honor of a famous jockey with that name. Those hopes were dashed when young Garrison grew up to be 5-foot-10 and 180 pounds. As a player he was nothing special, hitting .262 with little power.

Tuna **Dave Heaverlo** P, 1975-81

A colorful reliever who spent his entire career pitching for West Coast teams, Heaverlo was usually known as Kojak because he shaved his head. He also was known as Tuna, though I don't know the significance of that nickname.

Catfish **George Metkovich** OF-1B, 1943-54

Metkovich was fishing on a dock one day when he stepped on a catfish and got one of the fish's sharp whiskers caught in his foot. He needed surgery to get the whisker removed, and from that day on he was known as Catfish. Metkovich played for six teams in his 10-year career, batting .261.

Crab **Jack Warhop** P, 1908-15

Warhop's nickname has nothing to do with crabs; he got it because he had a crabby disposition. A decent pitcher (3.12 lifetime ERA), he is best known as the man who served up Babe Ruth's first major league homer.

Steaks and Chops

Porky **Doyle Lade** P, 1946-50

A short, chunky reliever, Lade was given his nickname by Dodger announcer Red Barber. He spent his entire five-year career with the Chicago Cubs, compiling a lifetime record of 25-29.

Raw Meat Bill **Bill Rodgers** 2B, 1915-16

Rodgers got his nickname because he was an avid hunter. Sounds like a real macho guy, but he didn't play like one, hitting .243 with no homers during his career.

T-Bone **John Shelby** OF, 1981-91

I'm not certain about the origin of Shelby's nickname, but I believe it has something to do with the fact that his middle name was T.—just that, T. As a player Shelby was very fast and a good outfielder, but not much of a hitter, batting .239 in his career.

Fowl

Turkey Mike **Mike Donlin** OF, 1899-1914

Donlin was a terrific player with a .333 lifetime average, but he missed considerable playing time during his career while pursuing success in show business. His nickname most likely came from his distinctive style of walking and running.

Library of Congress

Goose **Leon Goslin** OF, 1921-38

A Hall of Famer and .316 lifetime hitter, Goslin had his greatest years with the Washington Senators. He excelled despite the fact that Griffith Stadium negated his power, as it did every home-run hitter's. In 1926 Goslin hit 17 home runs, all of them on the road. His nickname is primarily a play on his last name, but also something of a commentary on his prominent nose.

Duck **Joe Lahoud** OF, 1968-76

Most players with the nickname Duck get it because they tend to waddle when they run, and Lahoud was no exception. As a player his power was decent enough to keep him in the majors for 11 years, but his lifetime average was only .223.

Chicken **Jimmy Wolf** OF, 1882-92

Wolf spent most of his career with Louisville of the American Association, winning the AA batting title with a .363 mark in 1890. As for his nickname, the story goes that he gorged himself on chicken one day before a game, and then committed several errors in the contest.

Side Dishes

Spud **Spurgeon Chandler** P, 1937-47

How about some spuds? There have been several players nicknamed Spud, but the best were probably Spud Davis, a hard-hitting catcher for several National League teams in the 1930s, and Spud Chandler, a pitcher for the Yankees and the American League's Most Valuable Player in 1943. Chandler was used carefully by manager Joe McCarthy, never starting more than 32 games in a season, but his career record was an astonishing 109-43 (.717) with a 2.84 ERA. Like Sandy Koufax, Chandler quit on top, winning the AL ERA title in his last season, 1947.

Hot Potato **Luke Hamlin** P, 1933-44

In 1973, there was a corny but fun movie called "Save the Tiger" with Jack Lemmon; he won an Academy Award for it. Jack played a businessman whose philosophies were outdated, and he showed how he was still living in the past by spending most of the movie trying to recall the roster of the 1939 Brooklyn Dodgers. In one scene he's kind of lost in space for a moment; then he blurts out "Hot Potato! Luke Hamlin!" The recollection brings him about as much pleasure as anything in the movie. Luke (Hot Potato) Hamlin was indeed a member of the 1939 Dodgers, and '39 was his best season by far with a 20-13 record. As for the nickname, New York sportswriter Jimmy Cannon gave it to Hamlin because he fiddled around nervously between pitches, handling the ball like a hot potato.

Potato **Carlos Pascual** P, 1950 and
Little Potato **Camilo Pascual** P, 1954-71
The Washington Senators under Clark Griffith were the first team to extensively scout players from Cuba, and their finds included the Pascual brothers, Carlos and Camilo. Carlos, the older brother, pitched only momentarily in the majors, going 1-1 with a splendid 2.12 ERA in two starts for the Nats in 1950. Camilo, who came along four years later, turned out to be an ace, pitching for 18 years and winning 174 major league games. The legendary Senators scout Joe Cambria gave the Pascual brothers their nicknames. He called Carlos, who was on the small side (5-foot-6), Potato, and Camilo became Little Potato, even though he grew up to be five inches taller than his older brother.

Taters **Frank Lary** P, 1954-65
A star pitcher for the Tigers in the 1950s and early '60s, Lary was best known for his uncanny ability to beat the Yankees. One day he was filling out a menu on a railroad dining car, and instead of asking for potatoes, he wrote down "taters." That became one of his nicknames; he was also known as Bulldog and Mule.

Spinach **Oscar Melillo** 2B, 1926-37
Melillo wasn't much of a hitter (.260 lifetime), but he was one of the best-fielding second basemen of his era. He spent most of his career with the lowly St. Louis Browns. In 1927 Melillo contracted Bright's Disease, a kidney disorder, and the doctors put him on a diet consisting primarily of spinach. Spinach became one of his nicknames along with Ski, a name his teammates gave him because of his admiration for Chicago Bear football star Bronko Nagurski.

Squash **Frank Wilson** OF, 1924-28
Wilson was a modestly talented outfielder for several major league teams in the 1920s, hitting .246 lifetime. I don't know why he was known as Squash, but he sure didn't squash many baseballs. He hit only one homer in his career.

Tomatoes **Jake Kafora** C, 1913-24
A fill-in catcher for a couple of seasons with the Pirates, Kafora batted only .125 and then disap-

peared. They say he used to eat tomatoes with every meal. Not exactly a ringing endorsement for the nutritional benefits of the tomato, is it?

Pickles **William Dillhoefer** C, 1917-21

I guess pickles can't help you hit, either, because Dillhoefer batted only .223 in his career. He got the nickname because of his last name, not because of any fondness for pickles.

Condiments

Salty **Francis Parker** SS, 1936

Parker played only briefly in the majors, but he had a long career as a coach after his playing days were over, filling in as an interim skipper on a couple of occasions. He was given the nickname Salty because of his fondness for salted peanuts.

Pepper **Jimmy Austin** 3B, 1909-29

A delightful man whose recollections were one of the highlights of Larry Ritter's classic book, *The Glory of Their Times,* Austin got his nickname because of his hustle and enthusiasm. Born in Wales, Austin got a late start in his baseball career but played regularly until he was in his 40s.

The Tabasco Kid **Norman Elberfeld** INF, 1898-1914

One of my favorite nicknames. Elberfeld was a small but feisty infielder for several major league teams, known for trying to disrupt baserunners with a shoulder block as they passed second base. Sportswriter Sam Crane gave him his nickname, a tribute to Elberfeld's spicy play.

Hot Sauce **Kevin Saucier** P, 1978-82

Saucier (pronounced soh-SHAY) was another colorful, feisty player. He was the hottest reliever in baseball for a short time in 1981, saving 13 games and recording a 1.65 ERA for Sparky Anderson's Tigers. But the kick in the hot sauce gave out pretty quickly, and he was gone from the majors a year later.

Vinegar Bill **Bill Essick** P, 1906-07

Essick had a very brief major league career, going 2-4 with a 2.95 ERA for the Reds in 1906-07. He then became a legendary scout for the Yankees, signing Bob Meusel, Lefty Gomez, Joe DiMaggio and Joe Gordon, among others, to Yankee contracts. He got his nickname because the German word for vinegar is *essig*; Cincinnati, of course, has a large German population.

Dessert

Peaches **Roy Davis** P, 1936-39
We had some peaches with our breakfast; how about some for dessert after dinner? Davis, a decent righthander for the Reds in the late 1930s (lifetime ERA 3.87). He got his nickname as a child because of his extreme fondness for peaches.

Strawberry Bill **Bill Bernhard** P, 1899-1907

Bernhard didn't like strawberries to an excessive degree, as far as I know, but he did have strawberry-colored hair. He was a fine major league pitcher around the turn of the century, winning 116 games and going 23-13 in 1904.

Peach Pie **Jack O'Connor** C, 1887-1910
O'Connor, who played for 21 years in the majors, got his nickname because he'd once played for an amateur team in St. Louis known as the Peach Pies. O'Connor managed the Browns for one season after his career was over, but lost his job when it was discovered that he was part of an awkward plot to deny the 1910 AL batting title to Ty Cobb. O'Connor told his third baseman to play on the edge of the outfield grass during his team's season-ending doubleheader with the Indians, thereby allowing Nap Lajoie to bunt for hit after hit. O'Connor never again managed or coached in the majors.

Pineapple **John Matias** OF-1B, 1970
Matias, who played briefly for the White Sox in 1970, was one of the few major leaguers to come from Hawaii. The Sox sent him back there after he batted .188 in 58 games.

Pie **Harold Traynor** 3B, 1920-37
Until Eddie Mathews and Brooks Robinson came along in the 1950s, Traynor was regarded as the best third baseman in major league history. He didn't have much power, but he was an outstanding glove man and a .320 lifetime hitter. There are several stories about how he got his famous nickname, but most of them revolve around his fondness for eating pie.

Gary Carter's Favorite Nicknames

The Kid **Gary Carter**
"My first big league spring training, I was allowed to watch the veterans play cards until Mike Torrez said, 'Kid, why don't you go get us some ice cream.' The name stuck after that."

Lights **Elias Sosa**
" 'The lights are on, and nobody is home.' He was clueless.

"They would give the attendance on radio at Olympic Stadium around the sixth inning. Sosa was a late reliever and would go to the bullpen around the seventh. They would put five attendances on the board, and then they would bet. He would always lose."

Hawk **Andre Dawson**
"He was as graceful as a. . ."

Spaceman **Bill Lee**
"Because he *was* a spaceman. But intelligent."

Rock **Tim Raines**
"Because he had rock hands, he became an outfielder."

Former Expos catching great Gary Carter is in his third season as the club's television analyst.

Politically Incorrect

Baseball nicknames are not always ideal for those with sensitive ears. Some examples:

Filipino **Dave Altizer** INF, 1906-11

Altizer, a run-of-the-mill utilityman for several major league clubs, got his nickname not because he was from the Philippines but because he had been stationed there while serving in the Army.

Wop	**Jim Pagliaroni** C, 1955-69
Dago	**Frank Quilici** INF, 1965-70
The Big Dago	**Joe DiMaggio** OF, 1936-61

Terms of affection? Yes, actually. DiMaggio was called The Big Dago by some of his Yankee teammates, many of whom were Italian themselves. Quilici, who was also known as Guido, was given the nickname Dago by a fellow Paisano, Twins coach Billy Martin. We don't know who hung the name Wop on power-hitting catcher Jim Pagliaroni, but we suspect the story was similar.

Polack **Fred Baczewski** P, 1953-55

You still could get away with a nickname like this in the 1950s. Baczewski, who had a nice rookie season with the 1953 Reds (11-4, 3.64), was given the nickname Polack by some of his minor league teammates.

Jap	**William Barbeau** 2B, 1905-10
Chink	**Earl Yingling** P, 1911-18
	William Wilson P, 1906

According to researcher Tom Shea, Barbeau was called Jap because of his diminutive size (5-foot-5 and 145 pounds) and swarthy complexion. Yingling got his nickname because his last name sounded Chinese, and Wilson was known as Chink because he looked Chinese. Wilson's career lasted for exactly one game with the 1906 Senators.

Superjew **Mike Epstein** 1B, 1966-74

Epstein was the most heralded minor league prospect of his day, and he was given his (hopefully) tongue-in-cheek nickname by one of his minor league managers, Rocky Bridges. Epstein's major league career was something of a disappointment considering the buildup, but he produced good power numbers despite playing in a succession of pitcher's ballparks.

Dummy **William Hoy** OF, 1888-1902
Reuben Stephenson, OF, 1892
Thomas Lynch P, 1884
Luther Taylor P, 1900-08
George Leitner P, 1901-02
There were a number of deaf mutes in the major leagues in baseball's early days, and most of them wound up being called Dummy. The best of them, by far, was the remarkable Dummy Hoy, one of the best leadoff men of the late 19th century. Only 5-foot-6, Hoy had a lifetime on-base percentage of .386 and scored more than 100 runs nine times. One of the most beloved figures in baseball history, Hoy lived to be 99 years old.

Nig **George Cuppy** P, 1892-1901
Jay Clarke C, 1905-20
Joe Berry 2B, 1921-22
Charlie Niebergall C, 1921-24
Johnny Grabowski C, 1924-31
Johnny Beazley P, 1941-49
I considered not mentioning this unfortunate nickname, which in every case was given to a white player with a very dark complexion. But let's not hide from it; this is part of baseball, and American history, as are the other nicknames in this section. The best player in this group was 19th-century pitcher Nig Cuppy, who averaged 24 wins per year in his first five major league seasons.

Jayson Stark's Favorite Nicknames

Eyechart **Doug Gwosdz**

Schnozz **Ernie Lombardi**

Fish Hook **Allyn Stout**

Piano Mover **Frank Smith**

Boom-Boom **Walter Beck**

Jayson Stark's favorite nickname story:

> "Boom-Boom Beck supposedly got his nickname as a Dodger. He got mad when Casey Stengel came to the mound to hook him and fired the ball off the right-field fence. The ball hit the wall so hard it had a boom, hence the nickname Boom-Boom."

Jayson Stark is a columnist for the *Philadelphia Inquirer* and *Baseball America*.

Nicknames of the Negro Leagues

The Negro League All-Nickname Team

MGR	*Rube*	Andrew Foster, 1910-26
C	*Biz*	Raleigh Mackey, 1920-47
1B	*Buck*	Walter Leonard, 1934-48
2B	*Bingo*	Elwood DeMoss, 1910-29
3B	*Judy*	William Johnson, 1919-36
SS	*Pop*	John Henry Lloyd, 1906-32
LF	*Turkey*	Norman Stearnes, 1923-40
CF	*CoolPapa*	James Bell, 1922-46
RF	*The Cuban Strongboy*	Cristobal Torriente, 1913-32
SP	*Satchel*	Leroy Paige, 1927-50
SP	*Bullet*	Joe Rogan, 1920-38
UTIL	*El Maestro*	Martin Dihigo, 1923-45

Great nicknames from the legendary Negro Leagues:

Impo **Dave Barnhill** P, 1938-48

Barnhill was a 5-foot-7 imp who threw the ball amazingly hard. He had his best seasons pitching for the New York Cubans in the 1940s, then played minor league ball for several years. Pitching for Miami Beach in the Florida International League in 1952, Barnhill went 13-8 with a 1.19 ERA. He was 37 at the time, and only his age kept him from a major league career after the color line was broken.

Cool Papa **James Bell** OF, 1922-46

One of the fastest players in the history of baseball, Bell compiled a .337 average in 20 seasons in the Negro Leagues. They used to say he was so fast that he could turn out the lights and jump into bed before the room got dark. There are various stories about how he got his nickname, but most are related to his coolness under pressure. Bell was elected to the Hall of Fame in 1974.

The Rope **Bob Boyd** 1B, 1947-50; MLB 1951-61

Boyd was young enough when the major leagues integrated to get a chance to show what he could do. He played nine years in the majors, batting .293. He got his nickname because he always seemed to be hitting line drives, or "ropes."

Home Run **Willard Brown** OF, 1935-49

A great slugger for the Kansas City Monarchs, Brown was one of the first Negro Leaguers to follow Jackie Robinson to the major leagues. Brown and Hank Thompson were signed by the St. Louis Browns in July of 1947, but when they failed to draw the expected crowds, both were released. Brown's .179 average for 67 major league at-bats gives no hint as to his real talents. He got his nickname after winning several Negro League home-run titles.

Pee Wee **Tom Butts** SS, 1938-50

Butts was a diminutive shortstop who weighed only 145 pounds. He was known for his great defense and was also a fairly decent hitter. Unfortunately the Baltimore Elite Giants star never got a chance to show what he could do in the majors, despite the fact that he was only 27 in 1947.

Tank **George Carr** 1B, 1920-34

A huge man who was built like a tank, Carr had his greatest years for the Philadelphia Hilldales. He batted .363 in 1925.

Hooks **Ray Dandridge** 3B, 1933-45

Dandridge was a solid hitter and an outstanding defensive third baseman for several Negro League teams. He was somewhat bowlegged and people said his legs looked like hooks. Dandridge was in his mid-30s when Jackie Robinson integrated the majors in 1947, and he had some huge seasons in the minors, hitting .362 for Triple-A Minneapolis in 1949 and winning the American Association MVP Award a year later. But he never got a chance to play in the majors. He was elected to the Hall of Fame in 1987.

Piper **Lorenzo Davis** 1B, 1942-50

Davis got his nickname because he came from Piper, Alabama. A smooth fielder at both first and second, he batted .378 in 1949 and .383 in 1950. Davis spent his entire Negro League career with the Birmingham Black Barons, serving as the team's manager during his last three seasons. Like Dandridge, he got a chance to play in the minor leagues and put up outstanding numbers, but he never was given a chance to play in The Show. He does have one claim to fame, however: he was the first black player signed by the Boston Red Sox.

Bingo **Elwood DeMoss** 2B, 1910-29

An outstanding glove man at second base, DeMoss was considered the best second sacker in the early years of the Negro Leagues. He also was a pesky hitter who almost always made contact. His ability to produce a steady stream of singles earned him the nickname Bingo.

El Maestro **Martin Dihigo** P-INF-OF, 1923-45

A native of Matanzas, Cuba, Dihigo was amazingly versatile. He excelled at virtually every position on the diamond, including pitcher. Hall of Famer Johnny Mize called Dihigo the best player he ever played against. The Cubans nicknamed him El Maestro because of his total command of the game. He was elected to the Hall of Fame in 1977.

Dizzy **William Dismukes** P, 1910-31

An early star of the Negro Leagues, Dismukes was one of the pioneers of the submarine pitch and is credited with teaching the pitch to Carl Mays, the outstanding submariner of the major leagues. Dismukes served as a manager and executive after his career was over. As for his nickname, the man wasn't dizzy; it was just a play on his last name.

Rap **Herbert Dixon** OF, 1924-37

A righthanded-hitting slugger who starred for several Negro League clubs, Dixon batted .382 for the Baltimore Black Sox in 1929. He came from the South, and his nickname was short for Rappahannock, a river in Virginia.

Rube **Andrew Foster** P, 1904-18

Considered the founding father of the Negro Leagues, Foster worked as a player, manager, executive and owner until his death in 1930. He got his nickname after defeating the great Rube Waddell in a 1902 pitching duel.

The Black Babe Ruth **Josh Gibson** C, 1930-46

Next to Satchel Paige, Gibson was probably the most famous player in the history of the Negro Leagues. He was indeed comparable to Ruth, both for the length and frequency of his home runs. Gibson was 34 when Jackie Robinson broke the color line by joining the Montreal Royals of the International League, but years of hard living had taken their toll. He died of a stroke at age 35 in January of 1947, three months before Robinson made his major league debut.

Rats **Arthur Henderson** P, 1923-29

Henderson had a short but outstanding Negro League career. A master curveballer, he went 19-7 for the AC Bacharach Giants in 1927—an astonishing win total for the short Negro League schedules. The 5-foot-7 righty eventually developed arm trouble, and his career lasted only seven years, all with the Giants. He got his unique nickname as a teenager, when someone left a rat in his lunchbox.

Crush **Christopher Columbus Holloway** OF, 1921-35

Holloway was a rough character, very aggressive on the bases, and an excellent leadoff hitter for the Baltimore Black Sox. There is some dispute about the name Crush: Holloway insisted that it was his real name, not a nickname, but other sources say his full name was Christopher Columbus Holloway. There's no dispute that he got the name Crush from his father. On the day his son was born, Mr. Holloway was planning to attend a fair which featured a stunt involving two locomotives crashing into each other. The birth of his son prevented him from going, so he called the baby Crush, either as a nickname or a given name.

Jet **Sam Jethroe** OF, 1942-48; MLB 1950-54

Jethroe was one of the fastest players of his generation, and the nickname Jet is a tribute to his speed. Jethroe was 29 when Jackie Robinson reached the majors, and he got his own major league chance with the Boston Braves in 1950. He responded by leading the league in stolen bases (a feat he repeated in 1951) and winning the NL Rookie of the Year Award.

Heavy **Oscar Johnson** OF, 1922-30

Johnson *was* heavy, a 250-pound behemoth who also swung a heavy bat. In his first three years with the Kansas City Monarchs, Johnson batted .389, .380 and .411.

Judy **William Johnson** 3B, 1919-36

An outstanding third baseman who was elected to the Hall of Fame in 1975, Johnson got his nickname because people thought he resembled Jude Gans, an early Negro League star. In his best season, 1929, Johnson batted .406 for the Philadelphia Hilldales.

Buck **Walter Leonard** 1B, 1934-48

Elected to the Hall of Fame with Josh Gibson in 1972, Leonard spent his entire career with the Homestead Grays. He was a teammate of Gibson's for many years, usually batting behind Gibson in the lineup. He got his nickname because his brother couldn't say "Buddy," which was the nickname Leonard's family had give him.

Pop **John Henry Lloyd** SS, 1906-32

The greatest shortstop in the history of the Negro Leagues, Lloyd was regarded as one of the best players ever by those who saw him play. Babe Ruth told sportscaster Graham McNamee that he considered Lloyd the greatest player of all time, and John McGraw once said, "If we could bleach this Lloyd boy, we would show the National League a new phenomenon." A .353 lifetime hitter, Lloyd managed various Negro League teams during the last decade of his career. He got the nickname Pop during those years as an elder statesman.

King Richard **Dick Lundy** SS, 1918-37

Lundy is considered one of the three greatest shortstops in Negro League history along with Pop Lloyd and Willie Wells. His strong arm and great range at short earned him the nickname King Richard. Lundy was also an excellent hitter, batting .409 for the AC Bacharach Giants in 1928.

Biz **Raleigh Mackey** C, 1920-47

If Josh Gibson was the best catcher in Negro League history, Mackey would rank a respectable second. All-around, he was probably the best, because he was an outstanding hitter (.322 lifetime) and a legendary glove man. Mackey is credited with inventing the snap throw to a base from his catcher's crouch. As for his nickname, the origins are uncertain. Mackey was quite a jokester, and it's possible he got the name from "giving people the business."

Gentleman Dave **Dave Malarcher** 3B, 1916-34

One of the few players of his day who had a college education, Malarcher got his nickname because of his all-around classy play and demeanor. Though better known for his glove than his bat, he hit .330 for the Chicago American Giants in 1925.

Ghost **Oliver Marcelle** 3B, 1918-30

Marcelle ranks with Judy Johnson and Ray Dandridge as the best third basemen in Negro League history. His career ended prematurely in 1930 when a teammate bit off part of his nose in a barroom fight; according to James A. Riley, Marcelle couldn't stand the razzing he got from fans and opposing players after the incident and decided to stop playing. Buck O'Neill says that Marcelle was called Ghost because he would disappear after a game and not resurface until the next contest. No one ever knew where he was.

Satchel **Leroy Paige** P, 1927-50; MLB 1948-65

Paige's fabulous pitching career and the origin of his nickname are covered in "Baseball's 25 Most Enduring Nicknames," but we couldn't leave him out of this section. Many regard him as the greatest pitcher of all time.

Double Duty **Ted Radcliffe** C-P, 1928-45

Still lively as he approaches his 97th birthday, Radcliffe got his nickname because he could pitch as well as catch. He got the nickname from sportswriter Damon Runyan, who had watched Radcliffe catch a shutout from Satchel Paige in Game 1 of a doubleheader, then throw a shutout of his own in Game 2.

Cannonball **Dick Redding** P, 1911-31

Big (6-foot-4 and 210 pounds) and hard-throwing, Redding got his nickname because of the overpowering speed of his fastball. He also used the "hesitation windup" long before Satchel Paige made the delivery famous. Exceptionally strong, he was capable of pitching both ends of a double-header or two or three days in a row.

Frog **Wilson Redus** OF, 1924-40

Redus was only 5-foot-5 and 155 pounds, and people thought he had a frog-like appearance. But the little man could hit, producing a steady stream of .300 seasons for the St. Louis Stars.

Bullet **Joe Rogan** P-OF, 1920-38

Rogan got his nickname because of his great fastball, but the compact (5-foot-9, 160 pounds) righthander had a huge repertoire of pitches. Along with a fastball and curve, he threw a forkball, palmball and spitball, and featured several different deliveries. From 1921-28, Rogan went 105-40 for the Kansas City Monarchs. When he wasn't pitching, he was a hard-hitting outfielder with a .343 lifetime average. Rogan was elected to the Hall of Fame in 1998.

Big Bertha **Louis Santop** C, 1911-26

One of the Negro Leagues' early superstars, Santop was a giant at 6-foot-4 and 242 pounds. He swung a heavy bat and hit giant-sized home runs, and fans called him Big Bertha after a long-range artillery cannon used by the Germans in World War I. Santop is reputed to have hit numerous "called-shot" home runs during his playing career.

Tubby **George Scales** INF-OF, 1921-46

Scales wasn't really fat, just a little bit tubby at 5-foot-11 and 195 pounds. A versatile player who could play anywhere on the diamond, he later became a manager and is credited with helping groom several players into stars, most notably 1953 NL Rookie of the Year Jim Gilliam.

Turkey **Norman Stearnes** OF, 1923-40

Stearnes was one of the great power hitters of the Negro Leagues, hitting as many as 24 homers in the abbreviated schedules of the times. James A. Riley credits him with 50 homers in 1924, including games against all competition.

He got his nickname because he used to flap his elbows like a turkey when he ran.

Mule **George Suttles** 1B-OF, 1923-44

Suttles was a big man who swung a 50-ounce bat and hit some of the longest home runs ever recorded. He hit 27 homers in 87 games for the St. Louis Stars in 1926. His nickname came from the kick of his big bat; fans used to yell, "Kick, Mule, Kick."

Big Florida **Ted Trent** P, 1927-39

A 6-foot-3 righthander from Jacksonville, Trent had his greatest years for the St. Louis Stars. In 1928 he had one of the greatest years in Negro League history, going 21-2 and then winning three more games in the playoffs.

The Cuban Strongboy
Cristobal Torriente OF, 1913-32

Torriente was the hitting star on one of the first great Negro League teams, Rube Foster's Chicago American Giants of 1918-25. He batted over .400 twice during that span. Also regarded as an excellent outfielder, Torriente was known as The Babe Ruth of Cuba.

El Diablo **Willie Wells** SS, 1924-48

A longtime star for the St. Louis Stars, Wells succeeded Pop Lloyd as the best shortstop in the Negro Leagues. Though only 5-foot-9 and 166 pounds, Wells hit with great power, belting 27 homers in 88 games in 1929. Also an excellent glove man, he became something of a legend during the years he played in Mexico, earning the nickname El Diablo (The Devil) for the way he robbed opponents of hits.

Shifty **Jim West** 1B, 1930-47

Though a big man (6-foot-2 and 216 pounds), West was a fancy fielder at first. Skipper surmises that he got the nickname Shifty because he was constantly on the move while fielding his position. West was talented but inconsistent as a hitter, batting .333, .215 and .422 in one three-year stretch.

Smokey Joe **Joe Williams** P, 1910-32

A 1999 Hall of Fame inductee, Williams had two nicknames which give evidence to his great fastball: Smokey Joe and Cyclone. Pitching for the New York Lincoln Giants during his greatest years, Williams was called a "sure 30-game winner" by Ty

Cobb, had he been allowed to pitch in the majors. In a 1952 poll conducted by the *Pittsburgh Courier*, Williams edged Satchel Paige in the voting for the greatest Negro League pitcher of all time.

Boojum **Judd Wilson** 3B, 1922-45

Wilson was a short (5-foot-9) but powerful lefthanded swinger who batted as high as .469 in a season. His lifetime average was .347. The nickname Boojum was an attempt to replicate the sound of his booming line drives as they hit off the outfield walls.

Craig Wright's Favorite Nicknames

Blue Moon **Johnny Odom**

Cactus **Gavy Cravath**

Downtown **Ollie Brown**

Icebox **Elton Chamberlin**

Oil Can **Dennis Boyd**

Other favorites are: Possum Whitted, Satchel Paige, Gates Brown, Kickapoo Summers (named after the Kickapoo Indian tribe), Stan "The Man" Musial, Ping Bodie, Chicken Wolf, Jazzbo Buskey, Bad News Galloway, Boog Powell, Bud Weiser, Mark "The Blade" Belanger, Half-Pint Rye, Bones Barker, Earache Meyer, Stick Michael, Butterball Botz, Cool Papa Bell, Ron "The Round Man" Northey, Flash Gordon, Steady Eddie Brinkman, Slow Joe Doyle, Cannonball Crane, String Grandy, Bullet Joe Bush, Swamp Baby Donald (also known as Swampy), Sudden Sam McDowell, Walter "Big Train" Johnson, Louisiana Lightning (Ron Guidry), Ding Dong Bell, Dusty Rhodes, Highpockets Kelly, Rainbow Trout, Leaky Faucet, Boob McNair, Goober Zoober, Puddin' Head Jones, Bow Wow Arft, Piano Legs Hickman, Wagon Tongue Adams, Glass Arm Brown, LP Mulcahy or Losing Pitcher Mulcahy.

> "I guess Mulcahy is my favorite nickname story. Hugh Mulcahy twice led the league in losses as a 20-game loser. He was named so many times as the Losing Pitcher that his fellow players started kidding him that his first name must be 'Losing Pitcher,' or in box score shorthand, he was 'LP' Mulcahy.

> "I also get a kick out of Icebox Chamberlin. He was called that because he was so cool under pressure. That just tickles me to know that type of characterization is as old as it is, and that his nickname is not likely to ever be used again because the icebox is no more."

STATS Director of Major League Operations Craig Wright is the co-author of *The Diamond Appraised* with Tom House.

Pun-Ishment

Think Chris Berman invented silly nicknames? Fuhgettaboutit. ESPN's nickname wizard had nothing to do with the names listed here, and many of these players got their nicknames long before Chris was even born.

Bill (Arbie) Dam OF, 1909

Good one, but why not Albie? Or God? Whatever. . . Bill Dam's nickname is a lot more memorable than his one-game major league career with the 1909 Braves (though he did go 1-for-2 with a walk).

William (Pickles) Dillhoefer C, 1917-21

Again, a name much better than the career (.223 with no homers in 600 at-bats).

Bob (Ach) Duliba P, 1959-67

From the German beerhall classic "Ach Der Lieber Augustine." Duliba, a pretty good reliever for several major league clubs, never played in St. Augustine, but he did pitch in Peoria, where manager Whitey Kurowski hung this nickname on him.

Roy (Slippery) Ellam SS, 1909-18

It would have been wonderful if Ellam had been a spitball pitcher who used slippery elm to produce saliva. But alas, he was a shortstop. And what a weird career. In 1909, he got into 10 games with the Reds and batted .190. He then went back to the minors for nine years. Resurfacing with the 1918 Pirates, he still hadn't learned to hit (.130 in 77 AB), and that was it for him.

Johnny (Whiz) Gee P, 1939-46

Until Randy Johnson came along, Gee was the tallest player in major league history at 6-foot-9. His height kept him out of World War II, but he couldn't take advantage of the opportunity to play against weaker competition (7-12, 4.41 lifetime).

George (Pickles) Gerken OF, 1927-28

Apparently, if your name is Pickles, it means you can't hit. Gerken batted .225 with no homers in two seasons with the Indians.

Bill (Smoke) Herring P, 1915

Herring's name was much more notable than his three-game career for Brooklyn of the Federal League in 1915.

Hitters smoked him for a .385 average and five earned runs in three innings.

Johnny (Hippity) Hopp 1B-OF, 1939-52

Hippity Hopp could hit: .296 lifetime. Hopp had pretty good speed, also, meaning that Hippity must have beaten out a lot of high hoppers.

Lyle (Punch) Judy 2B, 1935

A "punch-and-judy" hitter is a guy with no power, and that perfectly describes Lyle Judy's major league career. Judy got 11 at-bats for the 1935 Cardinals, and he's still looking for that first major league hit.

Laurin (Salty) Pepper P, 1954-57

One of the many 1950s bonus babies who didn't pan out, Pepper worked parts of four seasons with the Pirates, going 2-8 with a 7.06 ERA. At least he had a cool nickname, one given him by teammate Eddie Pellagrini.

William (Pol) Perritt P, 1912-21

When I was a boy, there was a brand of children's shoes named Pol Parrot. The commercials featured a kid who used to sing this song to a cartoon parrot:

Pol Parrot, Pol Parrot
Are the shoes you want to buy
They make your feet run faster
As fast as Pol can fly

No word on how fast *this* Pol Perritt could fly, but he was a pretty good pitcher (92-78 lifetime with a 2.89 ERA). Also, how fast *can* parrots fly?

Henry (Cotton) Pippen P, 1936-40

Scottie Pippen, this might have been you. Henry Pippen got his nickname not only because of his last name, but because he had very light-colored hair. Too bad he couldn't pitch (5-16, 6.38 lifetime).

Ron (Do It) Pruitt C-OF, 1975-83

At last, a modern ballplayer! This name fit Ron Pruitt perfectly, because he would do just about anything on a dare. According to Jim Skipper, Pruitt once wore a conehead mask on his head during the National Anthem.

George (Scissors) Shears P, 1912

Another great nickname wasted on a nondescript ballplayer. Scissors Shears had a 5.40 ERA in his four-game career with the 1912 Yankees. I like to think that his best pitch was the cut fastball.

Bob (Steamer) Stanley P, 1977-89

Another modern player, and a fine pitcher with the Red Sox for 13 years. We won't talk about Mookie Wilson or Bill Buckner.

Zack (Buck) Wheat OF, 1909-27

Like Goose Goslin, this was a great nickname for a great player. Zack Wheat spent his entire 19-year career with the Dodgers, batted .317 lifetime and was elected to the Hall of Fame in 1959.

Denny Matthews' Favorite Nicknames

Eyechart **Doug Gwosdz**

The Man **Stan Musial**

Blazer **Don Blasingame**
"When I was kid, he was my favorite."

Vinegar Bend **Wilmer Mizell**

Puddin' Head **Willie Jones**

Denny Matthews' favorite nickname stories:

"When Rocky Colavito was a coach with the Royals, he threw batting practice without much control. The players called him Lucky Strike.

"Former pitcher and coach Art Fowler walked with his feet pointed out. The players nicknamed him 10 'Til 2."

The longtime radio voice of the Royals, Denny Matthews has been broadcasting Kansas City games since the Royals' first season, 1969.

Place Hitters
(and Pitchers)

"Place nicknames" usually refer to a player's hometown or place of birth. The Commerce Comet (Mickey Mantle). The Springfield Rifle (Vic Raschi). The Manassa Mauler (Jack Dempsey. . . sorry; just making sure you were paying attention). You could also describe these as "newspaper nicknames;" they almost always were invented by sportswriters, and they almost always were nicknames which were used only in print. That is to say, no one ever came up to Mickey Mantle and said, "Hey, Commerce Comet." They're still fun, though long out of vogue. In a way, that's too bad. If we still had place nicknames in 1999, we might have these, all based on the towns the players were born in:

Modern-Day Place Nicknames

The St. Michaels Archangel	**Harold Baines**
The Shreveport Steamer	**Albert Belle**
The Riverside Ripper	**Barry Bonds**
The Oakland Out Man	**Dennis Eckersley**
The Sebring Saver	**Tom Gordon**
The DeLand Delight	**Chipper Jones**
The Hackensack Hacker	**Eric Karros**
The Pomona Pounder	**Mark McGwire**
The Tulare Traveler	**Mike Morgan**
The Melbourne Medicine Man	**Tim Wakefield**

Way cool. . . especially The Pomona Pounder. I may have some T-shirts made. Anyway, on to some real place nicknames:

The Hammond Hummer **Bob Anderson** P, 1957-63

A curveballing righthander who spent most of his career with the Cubs, Anderson was actually born in East Chicago, Indiana, not Hammond. But Hammond is right next door, and face it, The East Chicago Hummer is not nearly as cool a nickname.

The Cornhusker Express **Richie Ashburn** OF, 1948-62

The Phillies' Hall of Fame center fielder was—big surprise here—a native of Tilden, Nebraska. Ashburn had two other nicknames: Whitey, for his blond hair, and Put-Put, a nickname given him by Ted Williams because he was always in motion. "That Put-Put has twin motors in his pants," Williams said of Ashburn.

The Duke of Tralee **Roger Bresnahan** C, 1897-1915

Records indicate that Bresnahan was born in Toledo, Ohio, but he always insisted that his real place of birth was Tralee, Scotland. So he became the Duke of Tralee, and that's a good thing; as in the case of Bob Anderson, this is a far more romantic nickname than the Duke of Toledo. Bresnahan made the Hall of Fame primarily because of his reputation as a great catcher, but he caught more than 100 games in only one season, 1908. I guess when you're a duke from a foreign country, they give you the benefit of the doubt.

Tioga George **George Burns** 1B, 1914-29

In the teens and early '20s, there were two George Burnses in baseball, not to mention the one in show business. It was all pretty confusing, so to tell them apart, they called this one Tioga George because he lived on Tioga Street in Philadelphia. I forget which street George and Gracie lived on, but I'm pretty sure it wasn't Tioga. All kidding aside, Tioga George was a pretty good ballplayer and the American League MVP in 1926.

The Mississippi Mudcat **Guy Bush** P, 1923-45

Bush, who spent most of his 17-year career with the Cubs, was a native of Aberdeen, Mississippi. He is probably best known for serving up the last two home runs of Babe Ruth's career, but he was a fine pitcher with 176 career wins.

The Volga Batman **Mike Chartak** OF, 1940-44

I love this nickname. Chartak was American, but of Russian ancestry, and reputed to be a pretty good hitter. His major league career wasn't much; he was pretty much a wartime fill-in. But what a nickname.

The Kentucky Colonel **Earle Combs** OF, 1924-35

The leadoff man on the great Yankee clubs of the late 1920s, Combs scored more than 100 runs in eight straight seasons (1925-32) and was elected to the Hall of Fame in 1970. He was a distinguished gentleman who later served the Yankees as a coach. . . and as you may have guessed, he was a native of Kentucky.

Wahoo Sam **Sam Crawford** OF, 1899-1917

Classic place nickname here. A Hall of Famer and the all-time leader in career triples, Crawford hailed from Wahoo, Nebraska. He discussed Wahoo and his baseball youth at length in Larry Ritter's classic book, *The Glory of Their Times.*

Peekskill Pete **Pete Cregan** OF, 1899-1903

Another cool name. Peekskill Pete was no Pomona Pounder, though; he played only seven major league games and batted .095 (2-for-21).

Pea Ridge **Clyde Day** P, 1924-31

Day, a righthander with a marginal major league career (5-7, 5.30 lifetime), hailed from Pea Ridge, Arkansas. According to Jim Skipper, he committed suicide in 1934, three years after his major league career ended.

Peaceful Valley **Roger Denzer** P, 1897-1901

Denzer came from Le Sueur, Minnesota, which is where they grow those baby Le Sueur peas for Green Giant. The area is called—no, not the Valley of the Jolly Green Giant (though that would have been pretty neat), but Peaceful Valley. Hence Denzer's nickname. Denzer had two rather rough seasons in the majors (lifetime record 4-14), then presumably returned to the Peaceful Valley. At six feet tall, he was probably unable to land a job as one of the Giant's little pea-picking elves.

The Trojan **Johnny Evers** 2B, 1902-29

Library of Congress

I will studiously avoid bad jokes as to how Johnny Evers got this nickname. The real story is pretty simple: Evers, a Hall of Fame second baseman and the middle man of the famed Tinker-to-Evers-to-Chance double-play combination, hailed from Troy, New York. Only 5-foot-9, he also was known as The Toy Trojan. My favorite nickname for Evers, though, was The Crab. Originally he got this nickname because of the crab-like way he gripped a baseball, but it was totally suitable for a player known for his sour disposition.

The Bedford Sheriff **Elmer Flick** OF, 1898-1910

One of the lesser-known Hall of Famers, Flick was a .313 lifetime hitter who hit with power and drew some walks during an era in which offense was hard to come by. He hailed from Bedford, Ohio, but no one is quite sure where the Sheriff part came from, since there is no record that he ever served in law enforcement.

The Fordham Flash **Frankie Frisch** 2B, 1919-37

This is one of the most famous place nicknames. Frisch joined the New York Giants right off the campus of Fordham University and began a playing/managing career that earned him a spot in the Hall of Fame. The Flash part is a reference to his speed; he led the National League in stolen bases three times.

Harvard Eddie **Eddie Grant** INF, 1905-15

Like Frisch, Eddie Grant was a New York Giant infielder who got his nickname from the college he attended. Grant is more famous for something else: he served in World War I and was killed in the Argonne Forest in October 1918, the only major leaguer to die in that war. The Giants commemorated his death with a monument in center field at the Polo Grounds.

The Hondo Hurricane **Clint Hartung** P-OF, 1947-52

Also known as Floppy (see p. 151), Hartung was a much-hyped pitching and hitting prospect who never made it as a major leaguer. He came from Hondo, Texas. Both his nickames were much better than his playing career.

The Wild Elk of the Wasatch **Ed Heusser** P, 1935-48

Heusser was a native of Utah, living near the Wasatch Mountains. He broke in with the St. Louis Cardinals during the years of the Gashouse Gang, and his nickname is a variation on Pepper Martin's moniker, The Wild Horse of the Osage (see below). A pretty good pitcher, Heusser led the NL in earned run average in 1944.

Coldwater Jim **Jim Hughey** P, 1891-1900

Hughey came from Coldwater, Michigan, but as a pitcher, he was constantly in *hot* water. His lifetime record was a dreadful 29-80, including a 4-30 mark for the 1899 Cleve-

---

land Spiders, who were probably the worst team of all time. Hughey was bad even before he joined the Spiders.

The Goshen Schoolmaster **Sam Leever** P, 1898-1910

Some of these place nicknames are really cool, aren't they? Leever came from Goshen, Ohio, and he worked as a schoolteacher in the offseason. He was also a terrific pitcher. His lifetime record was 195-100, and he led the National League in winning percentage three times.

Year	W	L	Pct
1898	1	0	1.000
1899	21	23	.477
1900	15	13	.536
1901	14	5	.737
1902	16	7	.696
1903	25	7	.781
1904	18	11	.621
1905	20	5	.800
1906	22	7	.759
1907	14	9	.609
1908	15	7	

The Panamanian Express **Allan Lewis** OF, 1967-73

Charlie Finley had some very innovative ideas, but he also had some pretty wacky ones. One of them was to reserve a roster spot for a player who was basically nothing but a pinch-runner. Panamanian speedster Allan Lewis was the first A's player to fill this role. Unlike his successor, Herb Washington, Lewis could play the outfield in an emergency and had a total of 29 at-bats in the majors, with six hits. But his legs were his livelihood.

The Nashville Narcissus **Red Lucas** P, 1923-38

A pretty good pitcher (157 lifetime wins), Lucas was also one of the best-hitting pitchers of all time. He was frequently used as a pinch-hitter and had a lifetime average of .281. He lived in Nashville, Tennessee, and apparently had a bit of an inflated ego, which is where the Narcissus part comes in. What the heck; he could pitch, he could hit. . . why shouldn't he be a little stuck on himself?

The Pride of Havana **Dolf Luque** P, 1914-35

One of the first Latin Americans to play in the majors, Luque was born in Havana, Cuba. He won 193 games in his 20-year career and posted a 27-8 mark in 1923.

The Commerce Comet **Mickey Mantle** OF, 1951-68

Mantle was one of the last baseball superstars to be given a place nickname. He came from Commerce, Oklahoma, and he could run, so there you have his nickname. I'm searching for something about Mantle that you don't already know, so I'll try this. Did you know that Mantle played all four infield positions during his major league career, including seven games at shortstop? He was strictly an emergency fill-in for the late innings, but he handled nine chances at short in 1954-55 without making an error.

The Dominican Dandy **Juan Marichal** P, 1960-75

Dominican righthander Juan Marichal pitched a one-hitter in his first major league start, and for the next decade, he was about as good as it gets. I can still see him with a smile on his face as he got the catcher's sign before going into that high leg-kick. Marichal had six 20-win seasons, but every time he had a great year, Sandy Koufax or Bob Gibson seemed to pitch a little bit better, so Marichal never won a Cy Young Award.

The Wild Horse of the Osage **Pepper Martin** OF-3B, 1928-44

Martin was one of the more colorful members of the famed Cardinal Gas House Gang, so he was rewarded with a colorful nickname that paid homage to his Oklahoma roots. People tend to forget what a good player he was. Martin batted .298 lifetime, won three stolen-base crowns and scored more than 120 runs in three different seasons.

The Count of Luxemburg **Heinie Meine** P, 1922-34

If you've got a real name like Heinie Meine, I don't know why you need a nickname. But I have to admit that The Count of Luxemburg is a pretty nifty name. None of that Duke of Tralee foreigner stuff here. . . the Luxemburg in question was Luxemburg, Missouri. Meine led the National League in wins with 19 in 1931.

Vinegar Bend **Wilmer Mizell** P, 1952-62

Mizell was born in Leakesville, Mississippi, then moved to Vinegar Bend, the town that gave him his nickname. A pretty good pitcher, he won 90 major league games, then took up politics and became a U.S. congressman.

The Gause Ghost **Jo-Jo Moore** OF, 1930-41

The leadoff man on the Giants' pennant-winning clubs of the 1930s, Moore hailed from Gause, Texas. Don't know where the "Ghost" part came from, but the name has a nice ring to it.

Alabama Blossom **Guy Morton** P, 1914-24

A righthander who spent his entire career with the Indians, winning 98 games, Morton was born in Vernon, Alabama. His son Guy Jr., better known as Moose, made it to the majors with the 1954 Red Sox. Moose didn't blossom, however; in his only major league at-bat, he struck out.

The Knight of Kennett Square **Herb Pennock** P, 1912-34

Pennock hailed from Kennett Square, Pennsylvania, a very classy community where people raised horses and went fox-hunting. I have this vision of Pennock's chauffeur driving him to his first spring-training camp, then serving him a catered lunch on a white tablecloth; it probably didn't happen that way, but Herb was always a little classier than most major leaguers. Pitching for three great teams—the A's and Red Sox of the teens, then the Yankees of the '20s—Pennock won 241 games, then went on to become general manager of the Phillies.

The Gallatin Squash **Hub Perdue** P, 1911-15

Terrific nickname. Perdue came from Gallatin, Tennessee, and it was said that he was shaped something like a squash: a little on the portly side. He was 51-64 in five seasons with the Braves and Cardinals.

Gettysburg Eddie **Eddie Plank** P, 1901-17

According to Skipper, Plank was born in Gettysburg, Pennsylvania, attended Gettysburg College, worked during the offseason as a guide at the Gettysburg Civil War battlefield, settled back in Gettysburg after his playing career was over and died in Gettysburg in 1926. So I guess Gettysburg Eddie was a good nickname for him. A Hall of Famer who was a mainstay of Connie Mack's first Philadelphia Athletic dynasty, Plank won 326 major league games.

The Virginia Grapevine **Bill Quarles** P, 1891-93

We don't know which way Bill Quarles batted or threw, but we do know that he came from Petersburg, Virginia, and was known as The Virginia Grapevine because of his unique delivery. Apparently it was so deceptive that no one knew which arm he was throwing with. He pitched only briefly in the majors, recording a 2-3 record.

The Springfield Rifle **Vic Raschi** P, 1946-55

A hard-throwing righthander, Raschi was born in West Springfield, Massachusetts. He lived a shotgun blast away from the Springfield Rifle Company, so his nickname was a natural. Pitching mostly for the powerful Yankees of the late 1940s and early 1950s, Raschi compiled a splendid lifetime record of 132-66 (.667).

The Crabapple Comet **Johnny Rucker** OF, 1940-46

What an interesting nickname. Rucker came from Crabapple, Georgia, and he was extremely fast. He was a lifetime .272 hitter, with most of his action coming during the World War II years.

The Hoosier Thunderbolt **Amos Rusie** P, 1889-1901

One of the first great fastballers, Rusie led the National League in strikeouts five times. As you might suspect, he was a native of Indiana. Rusie won 245 major league games and was elected to the Hall of Fame in 1977.

The Naugatuck Nugget **Spec Shea** P, 1947-55

Shea, who hailed from Naugatuck, Connecticut, was definitely a nugget as a rookie in 1947. He went 14-5 for the Yankees and won two games in the World Series, including Game 1. He was never quite that good again, though he had a couple of decent seasons with the Senators in the early '50s.

The Dixie Thrush **Sammy Strang** INF, 1896-1908

Strang was a Southern boy from Tennessee and one of the first players to specialize as a pinch-hitter. A hitter with a good eye, he led the National League in on-base percentage in 1906.

Memphis Bill **Bill Terry** 1B, 1923-36

A straightforward nickname, just like the blunt and direct Mr. Terry. A lifetime .341 hitter, he remains the last National League player to hit .400 in a season (.401 in 1930). He succeeded John McGraw as manager of the Giants in 1932 and won three pennants in his first five full years as a skipper.

The Staten Island Scot **Bobby Thomson** OF, 1946-60

Thomson, whose pennant-winning homer in the 1951 playoffs is still probably the most famous home run in major league history, was born in Glasgow, Scotland. He moved to Staten Island, New York, as a child, and there you have the story of the nickname. His Shot Heard 'Round the World off Ralph Branca is so famous that you'd think it was his whole career, but Thomson played for 15 years and belted 264 homers.

The Earl of Snohomish **Earl Torgeson** 1B, 1947-61

Believe it or not, there were actually *two* Earls of Sno-homish. The first was Earl Averill, the Cleveland Indians' Hall of Fame outfielder of the 1930s. The second was Earl Torgeson, a fine first baseman with a good batting eye for several teams in the '40s and '50s. Pretty amazing, given that Snohomish, Washington, is a town of no great size. Averill's primary nickname was Rock, so we'll award the title of Earl of Snohomish to Torgeson.

The Arkansas Hummingbird **Lon Warneke** P, 1930-45

A good pitcher and a pleasant fellow from Arkan-sas, Warneke hummed his fastball over the plate well enough to win 192 games. The Hummingbird part might refer to his pitching, but it could also be a reference to the fact that Warneke sang and played guitar with Pepper Martin's Mudcat Band.

Eric Nadel's Favorite Nicknames

The Big Train **Walter Johnson**

Icebox **Elton Chamberlin**

Sudden Sam **Sam McDowell**

Blue Moon **Johnny Odom**

Shoeless Joe **Joe Jackson**

Eric Nadel's favorite nickname stories:

> "Dennis (Oil Can) Boyd got his nickname as a teenager because he drank so much beer, which they called 'oil' in his hometown.

> "Bucketfoot Al Simmons 'stepped in the bucket' on his swing.

> "Slidin' Billy Hamilton had over 100 stolen bases three straight years."

The radio voice of the Rangers, Eric Nadel has been broadcasting Texas Ranger games since 1979. He is the author of *The Texas Rangers: The Authorized History*.

Are We Not Men?

Players with feminine nicknames:

Lady **Charlie Baldwin** P, 1884-90

Forget the "Charlie" part; everyone knew him as Lady, probably including his wife (I'm assuming he was married). Baldwin got his nickname because he didn't smoke, drink or use profanity in an era when players were *expected* to be rowdy. Manly or not, Baldwin had a short but brilliant career, leading the National League in wins (42) and strikeouts (323) while pitching for the 1886 Detroit Wolverines.

Beverly **Bill Bayne** P, 1919-30

Beverly Bayne was a noted actress of the 1920s, and St. Louis Brown lefthander Bill Bayne got saddled with her name. At least we think so: Jim Skipper says he can find no mention of this nickname in contemporary literature. Bill or Beverly, Bayne wasn't much of a pitcher, posting a lifetime ERA of 4.81.

Ginger **Clarence Beaumont** OF, 1899-1910

A .311 lifetime hitter and the National League batting champ in 1902, Beaumont go his nickname because he had ginger-colored hair. He greatly preferred that name to his real first name of Clarence.

Sarah **Walter Bernhardt** P, 1918

Like Beverly Bayne, Sarah Bernhardt was a famous actress during the period in which Walter Bernhardt pitched. Sarah definitely had more than 15 minutes of fame, which is more than you could say about Walter. This Bernhardt's entire career consisted of two-thirds of an inning for the 1918 Yankees. But if it was a cameo appearance, it was a good one: Bernhardt retired both batters he faced.

The Darling **Amos Booth** C, 1876-82

Skipper, who would know, could find no explanation of why Amos Booth was known as The Darling. He didn't exactly have a darling career: Booth was a lifetime .224 hitter, he never hit a major league home run, and his lifetime fielding percentage at catcher, his primary position, was .746. That was bad even in the 1870s.

Kitty **William Bransfield** 1B, 1898-1911

A decent first sacker who played primarily for the Pirates and Phillies, Bransfield got his nickname because he wore his hair in bangs that hung over his eyes, a hairstyle that was then popular among women. He was man enough to bat .270 in a very light-hitting era.

Dimples **Clay Dalrymple** C, 1960-71

Dalrymple got his nickname from one of his minor league teammates, pitcher Joe Stanka. It's basically a play on his last name, but I've seen pictures of Clay, and he really did have dimples! All I can say is, if my last name was Stanka, I wouldn't go around giving other people nicknames.

Mary Ann **Al Doe** P, 1890

True story, courtesy of the amazing Mr. Skipper. During his minor league days, Al Doe had a teammate, Tom Cotter. A fussy type, Cotter had two bats which he called "Mary Ann" and "Mary Ellen." One day Cotter used Mary Ann to bang out a triple. Doe was the next hitter, and from third base Cotter yelled out "Mary Ann! Mary Ann!" meaning that he wanted Doe to use the same bat. The fans heard Cotter, assumed that Mary Ann was Doe's nickname and started yelling for Mary Ann to bang out a hit. Which he did. From then on, he was known as Mary Ann.

I have only two comments on this story:

1. Tom Cotter's nickname should have been Welcome Back, and

2. Did Doe have a brother named John?

She **Charles Donahue** 3B, 1904

Skipper says that in Donahue's day, She was a nickname given to players who had feminine characteristics, players who were thought to be homosexual or players who didn't smoke, drink or swear. Your guess is as good as mine as to which of these applied to Mr. Donahue, but one thing's not in dispute: She couldn't hit. In his (her?) one major league season, 1904, Donahue batted .215 with three walks and four extra-base hits in 200 at-bats.

Dolly **William Gray** P, 1909-11

Gray apparently got his nickname from the song "Oh My Darling," which refers to a Nellie Gray. His teammates thought the name was Dolly, not Nellie, and hung the nick-

---

name on him. No word on whether Gray liked being called Dolly, but he was used to misfortune. In three seasons working for the woeful Washington Senators, Gray went 15-51 despite a lifetime ERA of 3.52. When he went 2-13, 5.06 in 1911, it was Goodbye, Dolly.

Bubbles **Eugene Hargrave** C, 1913-30
Hargrave, a catcher who won the 1926 National League batting title, got his nickname because he stuttered and had problems pronouncing the letter B. He hated the nickname and would challenge anyone who called him Bubbles to his face.

Sweetie **Bruce Kison** P, 1971-85
When Kison joined the Pirate pitching staff in 1971, he was 21 years old but looked to be about 15. So the Pirates started calling him Sweetie. Kison may have looked sweet and innocent, but he was a tough customer and unafraid to pitch inside even as a rookie. In his first World Series appearance against Baltimore in '71, he hit three Oriole hitters and helped turn the momentum of the Series. He went on to have a solid 15-year major league career.

Little Eva **Bill Lange** OF, 1893-99
It's said that Lange got his nickname because people thought he walked like a girl. Is that why they called this decade "The Gay Nineties"? In truth there wasn't much girlish about Lange, who batted .330 in a short but spectacular seven-year career. Lange was only 28 and still at the peak of his talents when he quit baseball to marry the daughter of a wealthy San Francisco real estate magnate; the bride's father refused to let her marry a ballplayer, and that was that. The Langes eventually got divorced, but by then it was too late for Little Eva to make a comeback.

Cuddles **Clarence Marshall** P, 1946-50
Marshall got his nickname courtesy of Yankee teammate Joe Page. The New York writers were anxious to give him a nickname to replace his real first name of Clarence, and Page told him how Marshall had gotten mobbed by a bunch of teenage girls in the Yankees' hotel lobby. "They all think he's cuddly," suggested Joe. From then on, Cuddles was Marshall's nickname.

Grandma **Johnny Murphy** P, 1932-47
One of the pioneer relief stars, Murphy led the American League in saves four times while pitching for the Yankees. Teammate Pat Malone hung

the nickname Grandma on him. It seemed that Murphy always was fussing about meals and service, and Malone thought he was behaving like an old grandmother.

Honey **John Romano** C, 1958-67

Romano, a power-hitting catcher who had several good years for the White Sox and Indians, got his nickname when he was a baby. "Isn't he a honey?" his family members used to say, and the name stuck. Romano was a honey of a hitter from 1960 to 1962, averaging 22 homers a year for the Tribe.

Pussy **Charles Tebeau** OF, 1895

There were several Tebeaus in the major leagues in the late 1890s, and two of them had great nicknames. It's not completely clear how either White Wings or Pussy Tebeau got their nicknames, although Skipper points out that "White Wings" was a 19th-century term used for garbage collectors. As for Pussy, who was no relation, no one knows how he got his nickname, but he had an interesting major league career: two games, six at-bats, three hits, a lifetime .500 average.

Mother **Walter Watson** P, 1887

There is no information on which way Walter Watson batted or threw, but we do know that he played in two games for the Cincinnati Reds of the American Association in 1887. . . and that his nickname was Mother. As was the case with the nickname She, Skipper says that Mother was a name given to players who didn't smoke, drink or brawl, and that Mother was known as a real gentleman. Despite his clean living, he died at age 33 in 1898.

Peaches **Johnny Werhas** 3B, 1964-67

Third baseman Johnny Werhas played ball at the University of Southern California, under legendary coach Rod Dedeaux. The Trojans were playing the U.S. Marine team from Camp Pendleton one day when a fight broke out. Somehow Werhas got spiked and needed several stitches in his knee. There was another game the next day, and when Werhas showed some effects from the injury, the Marines began teasing him, yelling "Are you all right, Peaches?" Dedeaux—not exactly Mr. Sensitivity here—picked it up and started calling Werhas by that name, also. Werhas eventually made it to the major leagues, but Peaches' bat was definitely *not* all right. In 168 big league at-bats, he hit .173.

Rob Neyer's Favorite Nicknames

Little Hurt **Craig Grebeck**

Line Drive **Lynn Nelson**
"A 1930s pitcher who gave up a lot of them."

Ninety-Six **Bill Voiselle**

Jumping Joe **Joe Dugan**
"He wasn't a great leaper, but he frequently went AWOL from his team."

Rapid Robert **Bob Feller**

Rob Neyer on player nicknames:

"I reserve special mention for Ted Williams, who was hung with *three* solid nicknames: Teddy Ballgame, The Kid and (my favorite) The Splendid Splinter.

"There's a long tradition of sportswriters inventing nicknames, and as something of a sportswriter myself, I thought I'd give it a try. So for two years now, I've been referring to Greg Maddux as 'The Smartest Pitcher Who Ever Lived.' Okay, so it doesn't exactly roll off the tongue. . . but if Arlie Latham can be 'The Freshest Man on Earth,' why not?"

Rob Neyer writes a daily baseball column for espn.com.

The Human Zoo

The All-Animal Team

MGR	*The Cricket*	Bill Rigney, 1956-76
C	*El Gato*	Tony Pena, 1980-97
1B	*The Beast*	Jimmie Foxx, 1925-45
2B	*Parakeet*	Tito Fuentes, 1965-78
3B	*Mad Dog*	Bill Madlock, 1973-87
SS	*The Octopus*	Marty Marion, 1940-53
LF	*The Crab*	Jesse Burkett, 1890-1905
CF	*The Gray Eagle*	Tris Speaker, 1907-28
RF	*Cobra*	Dave Parker, 1973-91
SP	*The Whale*	Don Newcombe, 1949-60
RP	*Angleworm*	Ted Abernathy, 1955-72
UTIL	*The Wonder Dog*	Rex Hudler, 1984-98

A rundown by species, sort of:

1. Pet Players

Bow Wow **Hank Arft** 1B, 1948-52
Arft's nickname is a play on his last name. As a player he was no star, but hardly a dog: though underpowered for a first baseman, he had a lifetime on-base percentage of .352.

Pooch **Clyde Barnhart** OF-3B, 1920-28
Barnhart was no dog, either, a lifetime .295 hitter in nine seasons with the Pirates. Curiously, the origin of his nickname is unknown.

The Cat **Harry Brecheen** P, 1940-53
If they'd had Gold Gloves back in the 1940s, Brecheen would have won several. His quick reflexes in fielding his position earned him his nickname. He was also an excellent pitcher, winning 133 games and posting a lifetime ERA of 2.92.

Bunny **Anthony Brief** 1B, 1912-17
A big star in the minors, Brief batted only .223 in 183 major league games. Even the speed that earned him the nickname Bunny wasn't very evident, as he stole only 17 bases.

Bird Dog **Jack Conway** INF, 1941-48
Conway got the nickname Bird Dog while playing for Wilkes-Barre during his minor league career, a tribute to the way he hounded the ball on defense. The Bird Dog couldn't hit well enough (.233 lifetime average) to earn a regular position in the majors.

The Toy Bulldog **Clint Courtney** C, 1951-61
Courtney was a small but extremely scrappy player, and The Toy Bulldog was a perfect nickname for him. He was also known as Scrap Iron and occasionally as Redneck; the man got into a few fights during his career, as you might have guessed.

The Big Cat **Andres Galarraga** 1B, 1985-
Like Harry Brecheen, Galarraga is a graceful fielder known for his cat-like quickness. But he's better known for his hit-

ting. Galarraga led the National League in batting average with a .370 mark in 1993.

The Kitten **Harvey Haddix** P, 1952-65

First the Cardinals had the Cat, then the Kitten. A lefthander like Brecheen, Haddix won 20 games as a rookie in 1953, then 18 a year later. It was his pitching similarities to Brecheen, not his quickness on defense, that earned him the nickname of Kitten.

The Wonder Dog **Rex Hudler** INF-OF, 1984-98

Hudler fashioned a 13-year major league career more out of determination than talent. He would play any position, handle any job, and his nickname was a tribute to both his colorful personality and his dogged determination. You could win bets with this one: in 1996, Hudler batted .311 and hit 16 homers in only 302 at-bats for the Angels, the only time he hit .300 or reached double figures in homers.

Poodles **Joe Hutcheson** OF, 1933

Hutcheson played only one season in the majors, hitting .234 in 55 games for the Dodgers in 1933. He got his nickname because people said his running style resembled a poodle's. That must have been something to see.

The Black Cat **Leo Kiely** P, 1951-60

Kiely had a curious career, spending most of the 1950s bouncing between the Red Sox and various Boston farm teams. In 1956, he was having so much trouble notching his first victory that he took to bringing a toy black cat out to the Red Sox bullpen with him. When he finally notched that elusive victory, his fellow relievers ceremoniously buried the cat in the bullpen. A year later he was back in the minors, but he won yet another ticket to Boston with one of the most amazing seasons ever: he won 21 games for San Francisco in the Pacific Coast League while working almost exclusively out of the bullpen.

Mad Dog **Bill Madlock** 3B, 1973-87

A four-time National League batting champion, Madlock had a bit of a temper. He got his nickname after a 1980 incident in which he hit umpire Jerry Crawford in the face with his glove, earning a 15-day suspension.

The Big Cat **Johnny Mize** 1B, 1936-53

Like Andres Galarraga, Mize got his nickname because of his nimble fielding, but it was his hitting which put him in the Hall of Fame. He won four home-run titles in his career and won the NL batting crown in 1939.

El Gato **Tony Pena** C, 1980-97

El Gato means "The Cat," and like most of the players with this nickname, it was a tribute to his quickness in the field. Pena won four Gold Gloves as a catcher during his lengthy major league career.

Doggie **Tony Perez** 1B, 1964-86

Like a dog who could bring home the bones, Perez always could bring home the runs. He had 12 seasons with 90 or more RBI, most of them with the Cincinnati Reds. His Reds teammates hung the nickname Doggie on him.

Old Dog **Lew Ritter** C, 1902-08

The exact origin of Ritter's nickname is unknown, though he was a bit old—26—when he reached the majors in 1902. As a hitter he was strictly a dog, hitting .219 lifetime with only one career home run.

Squirrel **Roy Sievers** OF-1B, 1949-65

The American League Rookie of the Year in 1949, Sievers got his nickname as a high-school basketball player. His teammates gave it to him because of the way he was always hanging around the basket like a squirrel around a tree.

The Hit Dog **Mo Vaughn** 1B, 1991-

Mo Vaughn is no dog, but he sure can hit. Vaughn was the American League's Most Valuable Player in 1995, when he led the league in RBI.

2. Bird Men

Partridge **George Adams** OF, 1879

Adams' entire career consisted of four games with Syracuse of the National League in 1879. The origin of his nickname is unknown.

Dodo **Frank Bird** C, 1892

Dodo Bird. . . a cool name, though it's not clear how much Bird liked it. He had only one season in the majors, hitting .200 in 17 games for the 1892 Cardinals.

The Gray Flamingo **Tom Brennan** P, 1981-85

Brennan had prematurely gray hair and a very odd pitching motion. He used to pause in the middle of his delivery with his left leg sticking straight out, making him look like a flamingo. He had only a so-so pitching career, with a lifetime ERA of 4.40.

Rooster **Rick Burleson** SS, 1974-87

Burleson's nickname was a tribute to his aggressive personality. He was a solid shortstop for 13 years in the American League, most of them with the Red Sox.

Cuckoo **Walter Christensen** OF, 1926-27

Christensen was a zany character who talked constantly to opposing players and umpires, turned cartwheels in the outfield and even read newspapers on the field during a game. The Reds loved his act in 1926, when he batted .350 as a rookie and nearly won the NL batting title. They grew weary of him a year later, when his average slumped to .254, and they exiled him to the minors. Christensen never returned.

Chick **Wilson Fewster** INF-OF, 1917-27

Fewster had an 11-year career as a utility man for several major league clubs. I don't know the origin of his nickname.

The Bird **Mark Fidrych** P, 1976-80

The first time I saw Mark Fidrych was at Comiskey Park early in the 1976 season. Fidrych, who was still unknown at the time (he had yet to join the Detroit rotation) was sitting in the Tiger bullpen, bouncing up and down and talking to everyone in sight. "Who *is* that guy?" I thought. We all found out pretty quickly. Fidrych already had his nickname by the time he reached the majors—one of his minor league coaches had hung it on him after listening to Mark imitate a bird—and his legend grew as people saw him smoothing out the mound, gesticulating wildly, "talking to the ball" (he was most likely talking to himself, or his catcher). . . and winning games, 19 in all. Unfortunately the strain of throwing 24 complete games caught up with Fidrych's young arm (he was 21 in 1976), and he won only 10 more games after '76. It sure was fun while it lasted.

Parakeet **Tito Fuentes** 2B, 1965-78

A long-time major league second baseman, Fuentes got his nickname because he was constantly chirping to teammates and opposing players. His son didn't need a nickname; when Tito's wife gave birth on the day the Giants wrapped up the NL West title in 1971, Fuentes named him Clinch.

Hawk **Ken Harrelson** 1B-OF, 1963-71

A master at giving nicknames to *other* players during a subsequent career as a broadcaster (see p. 26), Harrelson had a pretty good nickname himself. He was known as the Hawk because of his large nose.

Emu **Jim Kern** P, 1974-86

As a young pitcher with the Indians in the early 1970s, Kern used to keep his teammates loose by squawking like a bird in the clubhouse. Teammates Pat Dobson and Fritz Peterson dubbed him The Emu, "the world's biggest non-flying bird." The Emu squawked in American League bullpens for 13 years and recorded 29 saves in 1979.

Duck **Joe Lahoud** OF, 1968-78

Lahoud had an odd, duck-like way of walking and running, and his teammates gave him the nickname Duck. Lahoud hung around for 11 years despite a lifetime average of .223.

Ducky **Joe Medwick** OF, 1932-48

No one is quite sure how Joe Medwick got his famous nickname, except for the fact that he received it as a minor league player. One story is that a girl saw him swimming and remarked that he swam like a duck. Another story is that a girl saw him *walking* and said that he walked like a duck. A third is that a girl—the same girl, or someone else?—saw him make a great play and squealed, "Isn't he a ducky-wucky kind of player?" Whatever the case, he was Ducky from then on. Medwick hated the nickname and preferred to be called Muscles, which was a better tribute to his great hitting. A .324 career hitter, Medwick was elected to the Hall of Fame in 1968.

Sparrow **Bill Morton** P, 1884

Though his exact height is unknown, Morton was a small man who was known as Sparrow because of his diminutive size. His career consisted of two starts for the 1884 Phillies, both of which he lost.

Donald Duck **Marty Pattin** P, 1968-80

A successful American League pitcher for 13 years, Pattin did one of the best imitations of Donald Duck I've ever heard. He probably preferred his other nickname, Bulldog, which was a tribute to his tenacity.

Jaybird **Johnny Powers** OF, 1955-60

Strictly a bench player during his six major league seasons, Powers batted only .195 in his career. Jaybird is a variation on his first name.

Crane **Frank Reberger** P, 1968-72

Reberger was tall and thin, kind of like a crane. He spent five years in the NL as an undistinguished reliever.

Little Duck **Dick Schofield Jr.** SS, 1983-96

Schofield's father, Dick Sr., was known as Ducky, so it was natural that the son would be known as Little Duck. Neither Schofield could hit much—Dad batted .227 lifetime, son .230—but both fielded well enough to fashion long major league careers.

The Gray Eagle **Tris Speaker** OF, 1907-28

This famous nickname was a tribute both to Tris Speaker's abilities as an outfielder and to his prematurely gray hair. Speaker could do it all: he was a .345 lifetime hitter and one of the best defensive outfielders of all time.

Birdie **George Tebbetts** C, 1936-52

Tebbetts was a catcher who never could stop talking to his pitchers, the hitters or the umpires. His voice was high and squeaky, and the nickname Birdie was a natural for him. Tebbetts caught for 14 years in the American League, then managed the Reds, Braves and Indians for another 11.

Stork **George Theodore** OF, 1973-74

Theodore's nickname was a lot more distinctive than his brief two-year career with the Mets. He was known as Stork because he was tall and gangly, with a bird-like way of running. The fans loved him, but when you hit .219 with no power, it doesn't matter how good a nickname you have.

Owl **Bob Thurman** OF, 1955-59

Thurman was a Negro League veteran who finally made it to the major leagues with the 1955 Reds. The Reds thought he was 32, but he was actually six years older than that; Thurman had discreetly lied about his age in order to increase his chances of getting a major league trial. Despite his advanced years, Thurman stayed with the Reds for five years as a spare outfielder and pinch-hitting specialist. He was known as The Owl because of his large eyes, and a wise old owl at that.

Turkey **Cecil Tyson** PH, 1944

Tyson got his nickname as a minor leaguer because he gobbled like a turkey. Great nickname, but not much of a career: he came up as a pinch-hitter for the Phillies on April 23, 1944, made an out. . . and that was it.

3. Sea Creatures

The Crab **Jesse Burkett** OF, 1890-1905

Burkett was a 19th-century great who won three batting titles and had back-to-back .400 seasons in 1895-96. He wasn't exactly Mr. Nice, however; his constant battles with opponents, umpires and teammates earned him the nickname of Crab. When you can hit, they forgive you for stuff like that. Burkett was elected to the Hall of Fame in 1946.

Sea Lion **Charlie Hall** P, 1906-18

What a cool nickname. Hall had a loud voice that could be heard anywhere on the field, and he used to entertain people by barking like a sea lion. The Sea Lion roared in 1912, when he went 15-8 for the World Champion Red Sox.

Bluegill **Jim Hughes** P, 1974-77

In 1975, Catfish Hunter was at the height of his talents and the highest-salaried pitcher in baseball. Hunter got so much attention that the efforts of other pitchers, like Jim Hughes of the Twins, were all but forgotten. Minneapolis sportswriter Pat Reuss thought Hughes might get more attention if he had a fish nickname of his own, so he dubbed Hughes "Bluegill." Hughes went on to win 16 games that year, but he was no Catfish Hunter. His lifetime record was 25-30.

The Octopus **Marty Marion** SS, 1940-53

Marion gobbled up so many balls at shortstop that people swore he must have had more than two arms. The St. Louis Cardinal star won the National League MVP Award in 1944, almost entirely on the strength of his great fielding.

Oyster Joe **Joe Martina** P, 1924

Minor league legend Joe Martina came from the oyster country of New Orleans. He had only one season in the majors, but it was a satisfying one. Oyster Joe won six games and helped the Washington Senators win their first major league pennant. Then he went back to the minors, where he spent a total of 21 seasons. Martina won an incredible 355 games in all—349 in the minors, and those six with the Senators.

The Whale **Don Newcombe** P, 1949-60

Don Newcombe was always a big guy, but people didn't start calling him The Whale until he started getting really big toward the end of his career. Overweight or not, he was an excellent pitcher with a splendid lifetime record of 149-90.

Rainbow **Steve Trout** P, 1978-89

Steve Trout was the son of former major league pitcher Dizzy Trout, and to be honest, the son was probably dizzier than the father. So Rainbow was a pretty good nickname for him. Given his bloodlines and his talented left arm, his career was something of a disappointment. Trout did win 88 games in the majors, but his season high in victories was only 13.

4. Hooved Hitters (and Pitchers)

The Iron Pony **Sandy Alomar** 2B, 1964-78

Lou Gehrig, The Iron Horse, played in 2,130 consecutive games. So when California Angels infielder Sandy Alomar ran up a streak of 648 straight games, his teammates dubbed him The Iron Pony. Alomar had a 15-year career as a major league infielder, but The Iron Pony's main legacy will be as a sire: his sons Robby and Sandy Jr. both developed into All-Stars.

The Baby Bull **Orlando Cepeda** 1B, 1958-74

Newly elected to the Hall of Fame, Orlando Cepeda was the son of Puerto Rican great Pedro Cepeda, a legendary star who was considered the Babe Ruth of Puerto Rico. Papa Cepeda's nickname was The Bull, so Orlando became The Baby Bull. Some baby.

Goat **Alvah Cochran** P, 1915

Alvah Cochran's career consisted of one major league game for the Cincinnati Reds. He may not have been the goat, but he certainly wasn't the star, giving up five hits and three runs in two innings. As for his nickname, its origins are unknown.

Ox **Oscar Eckhardt** OF, 1932-36

Eckhardt's nickname undoubtedly came from his first name, Oscar, but he also was reputed to be as strong as an ox. Eckhardt had only a brief major league career, hitting .192 in 52 at-bats; that's a pity, because the man could really hit. In 14 years in the minors he batted .367—second-best ever for a minor league player—and won five batting titles.

Moose **Bryan Haas** P, 1976-88

How did Bryan Haas—6 feet tall and 180 pounds—come to be known as Moose? His father gave him the nickname on the day of his birth, certain that young Bryan would grow up to be a moose. He didn't, but he did become a 100-game winner in the majors.

Mule **George Haas** OF, 1925-38

Haas, the center fielder on Connie Mack's outstanding Philadelphia A's champions of 1929-31, got his nickname while playing in the minor leagues. It was a tribute to his strength and a work ethic that enabled him to play 12 years in the majors.

Hog **Jack Jenkins** P, 1962-69

Jenkins, who played briefly for the Senators and Angels in the 1960s, was given the nickname Hog by teammate Bob Chance, who accused him of hogging the spotlight. Kiddingly, I assume. Given that Jenkins never won a major league game (his record was 0-3), never recorded a save and never got a hit at bat, it's hard to see how he would have ever been in the spotlight.

Reindeer Bill **Bill Killefer** C, 1909-21
Though not much of a hitter (.238 lifetime), Killefer was good enough behind the plate to last 13 years in the majors. His nickname is a somewhat tongue-in-cheek reference to his lack of speed on the bases.

The Bull **Greg Luzinski** OF, 1970-84
Greg Luzinski and I went to the same high school, Notre Dame High in Niles, Illinois, and he and I share every significant batting record in ND history. He was The Bull, I was The Brain. . . not. Actually, the only part of this story that's true is that Luzinski did indeed attend Notre Dame High a couple of years after me. The nickname came a little bit later, but it was perfect for a guy who grew to be 6-foot-1 and about 250 pounds. The Bull hit 307 major league home runs, most of them for the Phillies.

Citation **Lloyd Merriman** OF, 1949-55
One of the fastest players of his day, Merriman was named in honor of the great horse who won the Triple Crown in 1948. Ah, but you can't steal first base, and Merriman, whose lifetime average was .242, never could land an everyday job in the majors, much less win a Triple Crown.

Horse **Dale Mohorcic** P, 1986-90
The nickname is basically a play on Mohorcic's last name, but at times he did appear to be strong as a horse. As a rookie in 1986, he pitched in 12 straight games.

Hoss **Charley Radbourn** P, 1881-91
Radbourn, a Hall of Famer who won 309 major league games, was a Hoss who was always ready to be ridden. In 1884 he won 59 games for the Providence Grays, the most wins ever recorded by a pitcher in a single season.

Porky **Hal Reniff** P, 1961-67
Reniff, who broke in as a rookie reliever with the mighty 1961 Yankees, had several fine years, including an 18-save season in 1963. He liked to eat, and his teammates dubbed him Porky.

Racehorse **Charlie Robertson** P, 1919-28

Robertson, who threw a perfect game for the White Sox in 1922, wasn't known as Racehorse because he was fast on the bases. It wasn't a reference to his great fastball, either. He got the name because he had a long, flat nose. He also had a pretty flat career after the perfect game, which he tossed as a rookie. His lifetime record was 49-80.

Pony **Jimmy Ryan** OF, 1885-1903

Ryan, a Cub outfielder, is one of the best 19th-century players not yet in the Hall of Fame. He retired in 1903 with 2,502 hits, an outstanding total for an era when teams played much shorter schedules. Small and fast, he was known as The Pony Outfielder.

Old Hoss **Riggs Stephenson** OF, 1921-34

Stephenson got his nickname as a rugged football star at the University of Alabama. He was a terrific hitter (.336) for the Cubs in the late '20s, though his career was rather brief. He had only four seasons with more than 400 at-bats.

Piggy **Frank Ward** OF, 1883-94

Ward was a pretty good hitter for several teams in the late 19th century, batting .286 lifetime. He got the nickname because he was short and rather fat. Was there a Miss Piggy?

5. Bug Men

Angleworm **Ted Abernathy** P, 1955-72

One of the best relievers of the 1960s, Abernathy won two save crowns during his 14-year career. He was a submariner and got the nickname Angleworm because his pitches seemed to come up out of the ground.

The Human Flea **Frank Bonner** INF, 1894-1903

Bonner was flea-sized at 5-foot-7 and 169 pounds. An early utility player, he played for seven major league teams in six years.

Bugs **Tom Burgmeier** P, 1968-84
One of those lefty relievers who seemed to pitch forever, Burgmeier had his best season when he was 36, saving 24 games for the 1980 Red Sox. He inherited his nickname, which is basically a play on his last name, from his father.

Flea **Herman Clifton** INF, 1934-37
Clifton was fairly small at 5-foot-11 and 160 pounds. One of his minor league managers, Del Baker, thought that Clifton had the bite and tenacity of a sand flea, and that's where the nickname came from. He was strictly a flea as a hitter, batting .200 lifetime.

Ants **Fred Frankhouse** P, 1927-39
Frankhouse got his nickname from teammate Duffy Lewis. It was a reference to Frankhouse's nervous mannerisms on the mound. Nervous or not, he was a pretty good pitcher, winning 106 games in his 13-year career.

Spider **Johnny Jorgensen** 3B, 1947-51
Jorgensen won the Dodgers' third-base job as a rookie in 1947, hitting .274 for a pennant-winning club. Then Brooklyn traded for Billy Cox, and Jorgensen never played regularly again. He got the nickname Spider when he was playing basketball in high school. His team had black uniforms with orange stripes, and his coach thought he looked like a black widow spider on the court.

Mongoose **Eddie Lukon** OF, 1941-47
Lukon got his nickname from a newspaper article which said he was lying in wait like a mongoose. The Mongoose could lie in wait for a fastball, hitting 23 homers in 606 career at-bats.

Grasshopper **Willard Mains** P, 1888-96
Mains apparently threw underhanded, and the nickname Grasshopper was a reference to his style of pitching. He pitched for four teams in his brief three-year career, going 16-17.

Bee **J.R. Richard** P, 1971-80
Richard's nickname was a reference to his great fastball. He had more than 300 strikeouts in both 1978 and 1979, leading the National League in strikeouts each year. Richard might have had a Hall of Fame career had he not been felled by a stroke in 1980, forcing him into retirement.

The Cricket **Bill Rigney** INF, 1946-53

A New York Giant infielder who went on to a long career as a major league manager, Rigney was known as The Cricket for the way he hopped around second base. One of the first infielders to wear glasses on the field, he also was known as Specs.

Bugger **Frank Welch** OF, 1919-27

The origin of Welch's nickname is unclear, though it may stem from his middle name, Tiguer. Welch was a run-of-the-mill player, hitting .274 lifetime and losing his job as a regular when the A's started becoming a good club.

Grasshopper Jim **Jim Whitney** P, 1881-90

According to Jim Skipper, Grasshopper was either a reference to Whitney's oddly-shaped head or to his unusual style of running. As a rookie in 1881, Whitney led the National League in innings pitched, wins and losses, but his overall career record was under .500 (191-204).

6. Creatures of the Wild

Rattlesnake **Tom Baker** P, 1935-38

Baker grew up in the brush country of Texas, and he liked to entertain his teammates with stories about rattlesnakes. Unfortunately for him, his storytelling was better than his pitching for the Dodgers and Giants: Baker's lifetime record was 3-9. He did swing a pretty good stick, batting .310. Maybe it was all that practice hitting rattlesnakes with a stick.

Froggy **Joe DeMaestri** SS, 1951-61

DeMaestri got his nickname from White Sox teammate Al Zarilla. The reason for the name isn't clear, but perhaps it's because of the way he hopped after the ball from his shortstop position. DeMaestri was a slick fielder who played 11 years in the majors despite a .236 career average.

Bullfrog **Bill Dietrich** P, 1933-48

Dietrich was one of the first pitchers to wear glasses, and teammates thought they gave him a frog-eyed look. He spent almost his entire career pitching for bad American

League clubs; given his support, his 108-128 career record wasn't too bad.

The Bear **Mike Garcia** P, 1948-61

Garcia had sloped shoulders, long arms and a big, thick middle: a bear-shaped body, his teammates thought. The nickname also suited his competitive nature. Pitching mostly for the Indians, he recorded an excellent career mark of 142-97.

Rhino **Roy Hitt** P, 1907

Like Garcia, Hitt had a thick, strong body and a fierce competitive nature. He reminded his teammates of a rhino. Competitive or not, he couldn't pitch well enough to fashion a major league career. Hitt went 6-10 for the Reds in his only major league season, 1907.

Tiger **Don Hoak** 3B, 1954-64

Hoak was an amateur boxer prior to joining organized ball, and he was never shy about mixing it up. Dodger teammate Clem Labine gave him the nickname Tiger, but Hoak had his best years for the Pittsburgh Pirates.

Monkey **Pete Hotaling** OF, 1879-88

Hotaling was primarily an outfielder, but he also did a little catching. Researchers Bob Tiemann and Mark Rucker thought that Hotaling got the nickname Monkey while working behind the plate. He was a decent player, hitting .267 during the formative years of baseball.

The Iguana Man **Julio Machado** P, 1989-91

A Venezuelan reliever who had a couple of decent years for the Mets and Brewers, Machado got his nickname because he supposedly raised iguanas and liked to eat them.

Big Groundhog **Orval Overall** P, 1906-13

When you've got a name like Orval Overall, do you really need a nickname? I wouldn't think so, but the Cub righthander had one, and a memorable one at that. He got the nickname because he was an agricultural student prior to playing organized ball. Though he had a relatively short career, Overall was a terrific pitcher for the great Cub teams of the first decade of the 20th century. His lifetime ERA was an outstanding 2.23.

Cobra **Dave Parker** OF, 1973-91

Parker would have been a sure-fire Hall of Famer had he not gotten involved with drugs. Despite his problems he won two National League batting titles and an MVP Award while hitting 339 lifetime homers. His nickname refers to the way he uncoiled his powerful swing.

The Silver Fox **Jesse Petty** P, 1921-30

Petty, who was prematurely gray, was considered one of the smartest pitchers of his era. He couldn't have been *that* smart, because his lifetime record was 67-78.

Toad **Tom Ramsey** P, 1885-90

Skipper could find no explanation as to why Tom Ramsey was known as Toad. The name might have been a variation on his first name. Ramsey broke in with a bang, winning 38 and 37 games in his first two full seasons for Louisville of the American Association in 1886-87, but he quickly hit the skids after that.

Muskrat Bill **Billy Shipke** 3B, 1906-09

Another terrific nickname for which we don't know the origin. Shipke played a few seasons for the Indians and Senators, but a .199 career average prevented him from winning a full-time role.

Snake **Tom Sturdivant** P, 1955-64

Sturdivant's nickname was a tribute to his outstanding curveball. The pitch helped him win 16 games for the Yankees in both 1956 and 1957, but injuries derailed him and he was never again able to win in double figures.

Hippo **Jim Vaughn** P, 1908-21

Best known for being part of the double no-hitter pitching duel with Fred Toney in 1917, Vaughn had a fine career with 178 career wins. He got the name Hippo because of his lumbering gait on the basepaths.

Antelope **Emil Verban** 2B, 1944-50

Verban is best known as the inspiration for the Emil Verban Society, a group of dedicated Cub fans which included noted writer George Will. Verban was hardly an obscure player, however. He was a pretty slick fielder, and his lifetime average was a respectable .272. His nickname, Antelope, was a tribute to the graceful way he played second base.

Possum **George Whitted** OF, 1912-22

Whitted was a country boy and a dedicated hunter who liked to shoot opossum. Never a star, he was a decent player with a .270 lifetime average.

7. All-Purpose Animals

The Beast **Jimmie Foxx** 1B, 1925-45

Also known as Double-X (see p. 10), Foxx was one of the most powerful hitters in history, with 534 career homers. A beast of a hitter.

The Animal **Brad Lesley** P, 1982-85

Lesley was a huge man (6-foot-6, 230 pounds) who went a little crazy on the mound, carrying on like a wild animal in an effort to intimidate the hitters. He was much more famous than he was successful: he appeared in only 54 career games, with one win and six saves.

Ernie Harwell's Favorite Nicknames

Hill Billy **Emil Bildilli**

Climax **Clarence Blethen**

Death To Flying Things **Bob Ferguson**

Kiki **Hazen Cuyler**

Hippo **Jim Vaughn**

Hall of Fame broadcaster Ernie Harwell has broadcast Detroit Tiger games in all but one season since 1960.

Cartoon Characters

In many ways baseball players are superheroes, larger-than-life characters capable of doing improbable things. If they're *not* superheroes, they often have exaggerated characteristics, physical or otherwise—a little like cartoon and comic-strip characters, you could say. The relationship flows into their nicknames: several players have been given the names of cartoon characters. Some examples:

Goofy **Joe Adcock** 1B, 1950-66

A slugging first baseman who belted 336 major league home runs, Adcock was tall, strong and had a long face. He bore some resemblance to Goofy, the Disney cartoon character. But there was nothing goofy about the way he played. Bill James has written at some length about the Braves' misuse (and underuse) of Adcock, particularly under manager Fred Haney. Had he played under a more enlightened manager and in more hitter-friendly ballparks (199 of his 336 home runs were hit on the road), he might have had a Hall of Fame career.

Beetle **Bob Bailey** 3B, 1962-78

A former bonus baby who lasted 17 years in the majors, Bob Bailey was nothing like Beetle Bailey, the clever but lazy Army lifer from the comic strips. Bailey's best years came as one of the original members of the expansion Montreal Expos beginning in 1969.

Humphrey **Steve Bilko** 1B, 1949-62

Bilko was a big, slow-moving guy, and his St. Louis Cardinal teammates thought he resembled Humphrey Pennyworth, the big, slow-moving guy in the "Joe Palooka" comic strip. Bilko never got much chance to play regularly in the majors, but he was no palooka; playing for the Los Angeles Angels of the Pacific Coast League in 1956-57, he had back-to-back 50-homer seasons.

Skippy **Milt Byrnes** OF, 1943-45

Byrnes was named after the main character in a comic strip called "Skippy." He was strictly a wartime player, performing for the St. Louis Browns from 1943 to 1945 and then disappearing. He was only 29 in 1946, and you have to wonder why he didn't get another chance, as his offensive numbers were significantly above the league norm during his three years with the Browns.

The Jolly Green Giant **Bill Davis** 1B, 1965-69

A 6-foot-7 first baseman, Davis got his nickname when he was playing for the Portland team in the Pacific Coast League. As for his major league career, he apparently didn't eat enough spinach: his lifetime average was .181, with one homer in 105 at-bats.

Li'l Abner **Paul Erickson** P, 1941-48

Erickson was a big, strong, All-America boy type, and his Cub teammates thought he resembled the Al Capp comic-strip character. While no star, he was a serviceable major league pitcher with a lifetime ERA of 3.86.

The Roadrunner **Ralph Garr** OF, 1968-80

Garr, who was extremely fast, was named after the classic cartoon character created by Chuck Jones of Warner Brothers. In 1974 he treated National League pitchers like Wile E. Coyote, leading the league in hits (214), triples (17) and batting average (.353).

Flash **Joe Gordon** 2B, 1938-50

Any player named Gordon was apt to be called Flash after the futuristic comic-strip and movie-serial superhero. It was a particularly good nickname for Joe Gordon, one of the flashiest-fielding second basemen of all time. He could also flash the bat, belting 253 major league homers.

Wimpy **Mel Harder** P, 1928-47

The original Wimpy was a fat, hamburger-loving character in the Popeye cartoons. Many players who love burgers get the nickname Wimpy, as was the case with Tom Paciorek. Harder got it because he showed up in camp with  an unusually short haircut that his teammates thought made him resemble Wimpy. Whatever the case, he was an outstanding pitcher for the Indians, winning 223 games before going on to a career as a successful pitching coach.

Mad **Clyde Hatter** P, 1935-37

I can't say that every player named Hatter gets the nickname Mad, because Clyde was the only Hatter in major league history. It suited him because he was considered something of an eccentric character. And every time he took the mound, the hitters had a tea party: his lifetime ERA was 8.44.

Goldilocks **Hank Leiber** OF, 1933-42

Yeah, I know. . . Goldilocks was a fairy-tale character, not a cartoon character. But it's close enough. Leiber, who got his nickname because of his blonde hair, was a pretty good hitter, with 101 lifetime homers. Fittingly, Goldilocks spent a few seasons playing with the bears (Cubs), hitting 24 dingers in 1939. They thought he was a pretty good player, but they hated it when he sneaked into the clubhouse and ate all of Baby Bear's porridge.

The Cat **Felix Mantilla** INF, 1956-66

Felix the Cat was a pretty cagey cartoon character, so I wonder if he could explain Felix Mantilla's career to me. For years Mantilla was a utility infielder for the Braves who couldn't hit but was known as a pretty good glove man. Then he went to the Mets and Red Sox, where he started hitting like crazy (30 HR in 1964) while his glove went south. Finally he went to Houston, where he couldn't hit *or* field. Figure it out for me, Felix.

Mickey Mouse **Cliff Melton** P, 1937-44

Melton's most famous nickname was Mountain Music (see p. 7), but he was also known as Mickey Mouse—a reference to his big ears. His career was *not* Mickey Mouse. . . especially in 1937, when he won 20 games as a rookie.

Spiderman **Ben Oglivie** OF, 1971-86

Oglivie got his nickname because of his spider-like build: long arms, skinny legs. But his wiry body could generate amazing bat speed, and he belted 235 major league home runs, including 41 in 1980.

Humpty Dumpty **Mark Polhemus** OF, 1887

OK, Humpty Dumpty comes from a nursery rhyme, but I had to get this guy in. Polhemus is something of a mystery man; we know he played in 20 games for the Indianapolis club of the American Association in 1887 and batted .240, but we don't know which way he batted and threw, and we don't know how he got his nickname. Did he sit on the wall? Did he have a great fall? Nobody seems to know.

Foghorn Leghorn **Doug Rader** 3B, 1967-77

A slick-fielding third baseman who won five Gold Gloves, Rader really did look like Foghorn Leghorn, the blustering rooster from the cartoons. He had the same slanty eyes, the big head, the shock of red hair. Also known as The Red Rooster, Rader managed the Rangers and Angels after his playing career ended.

Sugar Bear **Floyd Rayford** C-3B, 1980-87

The Sugar Bear was a small, pudgy little character who appeared in Sugar Crisp cereal commercials. Floyd Rayford was a small, pudgy little utility player who looked like he'd been hitting the Sugar Crisp pretty hard. Despite his appearance Rayford wasn't a bad player; in 1985, the only year he played more than 100 games, he belted 18 home runs.

Buck **Bob Rodgers** C, 1961-69

In the movies and comic strips, Buck Rogers flew off to the heavens. How fitting, then, that one of the expansion Angels' first stars was catcher Bob (Buck) Rodgers. A good catcher but not much of a batsman, Rodgers later managed the Brewers and Expos.

Skinny **Wally Shaner** OF, 1923-29

One of the early comic strips was a strip called "Us Boys." It featured a character called Skinny Shaner, and it was natural that tall, slim Wally Shaner would be known as Skinny. Shaner had only one year as a regular, hitting .273 for the 1927 Red Sox.

Little Nemo **Jim Stephens** C, 1907-12

Another early strip was Winser McKay's "Little Nemo in Slumberland." Short and rather squat, Stephens was said to resemble Little Nemo. I wouldn't know, but I've looked at his batting record, and it was strictly Slumberland: .227 lifetime, with no power.

Bunky **Veston Stewart** P, 1952-56

Yet another comic strip you probably never heard of was one from the 1920s called "Parlor, Bedroom and Sink, Starring Bunky." In the comic strip Bunky was always getting into scrapes, just like little Veston Stewart. Veston's grandfather, a big fan of the strip, started calling his grandson Bunky, and the name stuck. Young Bunky Stewart grew up to pitch for the Washington Senators, where he was part of the starting rotation with Parlor, Bedroom and Sink. Or something like that.

Mutt **David Williams** P, 1913-14

"Mutt and Jeff" was one of the more famous comic strips. It featured the adventures of a really tall guy named Mutt and

---

a really short guy named Jeff. David Williams got the nickname Mutt because he was 6-foot-3, which was exceptionally tall for 1913. He didn't have many major league adventures, just six games with a 4.91 ERA for the Senators in 1914. Maybe the problem was that the Senators didn't have anybody named Jeff.

Ozark Ike **Gus Zernial** OF, 1949-59

"Ozark Ike" was a comic strip about a ballplayer, a big, strong country boy. Gus Zernial was a big, strong kid from Beaumont, Texas. In the late 1940s Zernial spent some time with the Hollywood Stars of the Pacific Coast League, and Fred Haney, one of the club's announcers, started referring to Zernial as Ozark Ike. The name stayed with him for the rest of his playing days. Zernial went on to a fine career with several American League clubs; he led the AL with 33 homers in 1951 and hit 237 in his major league career.

Popeye **Don Zimmer** INF, 1954-65

Now Don Zimmer. . . *there's* a cartoon character! As he got older, Zimmer started looking more and more like Popeye the Sailor Man; he didn't have the pipe or the spinach, but he sure had the look down pat. It's easy to make fun of him, but he's had a long and admirable career as a baseball lifer, bouncing back from adversity again and again. Nearly 70 years old, he's still at it, filling in this spring for Joe Torre as manager of the Yankees. Like Popeye himself, Zimmer has proven to be "strong to the finish." Count me as a fan of his.

Tim Kurkjian's Favorite Nicknames

Eyechart **Doug Gwosdz**

"Gwosdz got the name Eyechart from Doug Rader when he played in San Diego. Rader used to put one hand over his eye and say 'G-W-O-S-D-Z.' It's pronounced Goosh."

Mikie **Dave Hollins**

"This was not a well-known nickname except among the '93 Phils. Hollins, amazingly intense, got the nickname because of the little boy on the Life Cereal commercial: 'Let Mikie try it, he hates everything.'"

Tim Kurkjian is a senior writer for *ESPN Magazine*.

The Body-Parts Shop

The All Body-Parts Team

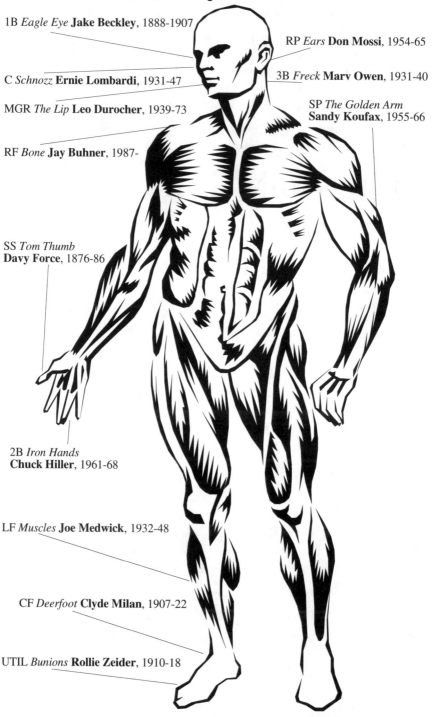

1B *Eagle Eye* **Jake Beckley**, 1888-1907

RP *Ears* **Don Mossi**, 1954-65

C *Schnozz* **Ernie Lombardi**, 1931-47

3B *Freck* **Marv Owen**, 1931-40

MGR *The Lip* **Leo Durocher**, 1939-73

SP *The Golden Arm*
Sandy Koufax, 1955-66

RF *Bone* **Jay Buhner**, 1987-

SS *Tom Thumb*
Davy Force, 1876-86

2B *Iron Hands*
Chuck Hiller, 1961-68

LF *Muscles* **Joe Medwick**, 1932-48

CF *Deerfoot* **Clyde Milan**, 1907-22

UTIL *Bunions* **Rollie Zeider**, 1910-18

Let's do the whole body of players, starting from the top of the head:

Pigtail Billy **Billy Riley** OF, 1879

Early stylin': Riley wore his hair in a pigtail. The fans probably loved it, but when you hit .145, even a cool hairdo won't help keep you around. After 44 games for the 1879 Reds, Riley was gone.

Curly **Ernie Ross** P, 1902

Ross was known for his curly hair. . . but not, alas, for his pitching. After two starts with a 7.41 ERA, it was curtains for Curly.

Baldy **Dick Rudolph** P, 1910-27

Unlike Riley and Ross, Dick Rudolph had very little hair. But who needs hair when you can pitch? One of the aces of the 1914 Miracle Braves with a 26-10 record, Rudolph won 121 major league games with a 2.66 ERA.

Brains **Dick Padden** 2B, 1896-1905

Padden was reputed to be a very smart player. I'm not sure whether this is a sign of intelligence, but Padden consistently ranked among the league leaders in being hit by pitches. Nothing like taking one for the team, eh, Brains?

Eagle Eye **Jake Beckley** 1B, 1888-1907

A star first baseman who banged out 2,930 hits, Beckley was elected to the Hall of Fame in 1971. Jim Skipper says that Beckley got his nickname because of his ability to distinguish balls from strikes, but he never drew more than 54 walks in a season. On the other hand he didn't strike out much, either.

Patcheye **Johnny Gill** OF, 1927-36

Skipper surmises that Gill got his nickname because he once played in a game while wearing a patch over his eye. However, he could find no documentation for this. Actually, Gill hit like he always had a patch over his eye, batting .245 during one of the heaviest-hitting eras in major league history. He did have a little bit of power, though.

The Human Eyeball **Bris Lord** OF, 1905-13

Lord's nickname, like Jake Beckley's, suggests a player who drew a lot of walks. As with Beckley, that wasn't the case with Lord, whose season high in walks was 35. So his nickname is a bit of a mystery. Whatever the case, Lord had some fine years for Connie Mack's first Philadelphia A's dynasty, hitting .310 for the 1911 World Champions.

Ears **Don Mossi** P, 1954-65

No mystery where *this* nickname came from. Don Mossi was to ears what Jimmy Durante was to noses, or Jay Leno to chins: Mossi's face, someone once wrote, looked like a taxicab with its doors opened wide on each side. Mossi was homely, to be sure, but he was also an excellent pitcher. He broke in as a relief star (with fellow rookie reliever Ray Narleski) for the American League champion Indians of 1954. Later he was switched to a starting role and won as many as 17 games in a season.

Rabbit Ears **Cliff Melton** P, 1937-44

Melton had three nicknames, all of them good: Mountain Music (see p. 7), Mickey Mouse (p. 132) and Rabbit Ears. The latter two nicknames refer to Melton's prominent ears. He wasn't quite Don Mossi, but he was close.

Bootnose **Fred Hofmann** C, 1919-28

A reserve catcher for the Yankees and A's in the 1920s, Hofmann was well known for his large, boot-shaped nose. He retired after compiling exactly 1,000 major league at-bats (with 247 hits), then went on to have a long and successful career as a minor league manager and major league coach and scout.

Schnozz **Ernie Lombardi** C, 1931-47

Lombardi had both a big nose and a big bat. He won two National League batting titles—a rare feat for a catcher—and batted .306 during his career. Since Lombardi was regarded as one of the slowest runners in history, that .306 average is even more impressive. He was elected to the Hall of Fame in 1986.

Horn **Ed Sauer** OF, 1943-49 and
The Honker **Hank Sauer** OF, 1941-59

The Sauer brothers were National League outfielders of the 1940s, both known for their exceptionally large noses. Ed wasn't much of a player (.256 with five lifetime homers), but Hank was a lot more than just a guy with a big schnozzola. Though the Reds didn't give him his first real major league chance until he was 31 years old, Sauer managed to hit 288 home runs in The Show.

The Lip **Leo Durocher** SS, 1925-45

Durocher joined the Yankees as a brash, talkative rookie in 1928, and his teammates immediately dubbed him Lippy Leo. Durocher was undeterred, and he was Leo the Lip for the rest of his long career as a player and manager. As a manager he was one of the best ever; as a hitter he was best described by another one of his nicknames, The All-American Out.

Smiley **John Bischoff** C, 1925-26

A reserve catcher with the White and Red Sox in the mid-1920s, Bischoff was known for his sunny disposition. He wasn't a terrible hitter (.262 lifetime), but Smiley disappeared from the majors after two seasons.

Grin **George Bradley** P, 1876-88

Bradley got his nickname because he always seemed to have a grin on his face whenever he was pitching. That must have been easy in 1876, when he had a 45-19 record and a league-leading 1.23 ERA for St. Louis in the National League's inaugural season. It couldn't have been easy three years later, when his record was 13-40, or two years after that, when his arm was going bad and he was playing for his fifth NL team in five years. Bradley survived, even playing third base for awhile, and in 1884, his last full year in the game, he went 25-15 for Cincinnati in the Union Association. No doubt it made him grin.

Smiler **George Murray** P, 1922-33

Another happy guy. Unlike Bradley, George Murray had hardly any success at the major league level, going 20-26 with a 5.38 ERA. I know *I* wouldn't be smiling.

Dimples **Edward Tate** C, 1885-90

Skipper, who knows these things, reports that Tate did indeed have dimples, but that he preferred to be known as Pop. As a hitter, Pop didn't have much pop, hitting .218 lifetime. But he did have those nice dimples.

Freck **Marv Owen** 3B, 1931-40

Owen was the third baseman on the Tigers' American League championship teams of 1934-35. The '34 Tiger infield was amazingly durable: first baseman Hank Greenberg missed one game all season, and second baseman Charlie Gehringer, shortstop Bill Rogell and Owen all played in every contest. Owen got his nickname because his face was covered with freckles.

Cheeky **Leon Wagner** OF, 1958-69

The colorful Wagner used to refer to himself as Daddy Wags, and even had an LA clothing shop with that name (his ads used to say, "Get Your Rags at Daddy Wags'"). Wagner had very high cheekbones, and Cheeky was a nickname hung on him by Giant trainer Frank Bowman.

Ol' Stubblebeard **Burleigh Grimes** P, 1916-34

A Hall of Famer and the last spitballer to legally ply his trade in the major leagues, Grimes won 270 major league games. He got his nickname because he never would shave on days he was scheduled to pitch. People thought he did this to give him a more intimidating presence, but the real story is a lot less macho. It seems that Grimes used to chew on slippery elm in order to produce more saliva, and his skin would become irritated from the slippery elm juice dripping down his chin. I personally think that Ol' Sensitive Skin would have been a really terrific nickname, but I can see where Grimes might prefer to be known as Ol' Stubblebeard.

Spittin' Bill **Bill Doak** P, 1912-29

Like Grimes, Doak was one of the last of the legal spitballers. He won 169 games in his career, but his main claim to fame is that he helped reinvent the baseball glove. The "Bill Doak Model," the first glove with a pocket and a web between the thumb and forefinger, helped revolutionize the game.

Salavita **Raul Sanchez** P, 1952-60

Sanchez was also reputed to have thrown the spitball, though not legally. The Cuban righthander got a few trials with the Senators and Reds, but was never able to find consistent success.

Tomato Face **Nick Cullop** OF, 1926-31

Known for his ruddy complexion, Cullop left more than a few pitchers red-faced. His major league career wasn't much (.249 in 490 at-bats), but he was a minor league legend, recording a record 1,857 RBI in the minors.

Square Jaw **Bill Ramsey** OF, 1945

As you may have guessed, Ramsey had a very square jaw. What he didn't get was a square deal. After hitting .292 for the Braves in 1945, his first major league season, he never got another chance, despite the fact that he was only 25 years old in '45.

Redneck **Clint Courtney** C, 1951-61

Also known as Scrap Iron and The Toy Bulldog (see p. 111), Courtney was colorful but hot-tempered. He had several main events during his career, including a legendary brawl with Billy Martin.

Shoulders **Tom Acker** P, 1956-59

Back in the 1950s, most players shied away from body-building and weightlifting out of concern that it would make them too musclebound. Acker, who had a well-chiseled physique, was one of the few exceptions. He had some decent seasons with the Reds, finishing his career with a 19-13 record.

Shoulders **Barry Latman** P, 1957-67

I try not to repeat nicknames in this book, but everybody needs two shoulders, right? Latman was another pitcher with a well-muscled body at a time when that was unusual. He was a decent starter/reliever, especially in 1961, when he went 13-5 for the Indians.

Chesty Chet **Chet Johnson** P, 1946

Johnson's nickname was more memorable than his career, which consisted of five pitching appearances for the 1946 Browns. He had an 0-0 record and a 5.00 ERA—not much to stick your chest out about.

Ribs **Frank Raney** P, 1949-50

Raney was tall and extremely skinny, especially as a teenager. He looked like the guy in the Charles Atlas ads who got pushed around by the bully with the body like Barry Latman's. You know, "Hey, Skinny! Yer ribs are showing!" As for Raney's major league career, he spent two years with the Browns getting sand kicked in his face (7.36 lifetime ERA).

Muscles **Joe Medwick** OF, 1932-48

Medwick, as we point out in "The Human Zoo" (see p. 115), much preferred being called Muscles rather than the moniker that was usually hung on him, Ducky Wucky. He had a great physique, and it helped him hit .324 and win a spot in the Hall of Fame.

Bones **Dick Tomanek** P, 1953-59

Another skinny guy, Tomanek pitched without distinction for the Indians and A's in the 1950s. His main claim to fame was that he was part of the deal that sent Roger Maris from the Indians to the A's in 1958.

The Arm **Tom Hafey** 3B, 1939-44

With a nickname like The Arm, you'd think Hafey would have been a pitcher. Instead he was a third baseman with an exceptionally strong throwing arm. He played briefly for the Giants and Browns, hitting .248 in 78 career games.

The Golden Arm **Sandy Koufax** P, 1955-66

Koufax got this nickname at the height of his Hall of Fame career with the Dodgers. He won ERA titles in each of his last five major league seasons, going 26-8 and 27-9 his last two years.

Rubber Arm **Gene Krapp** P, 1911-15

When your last name is Krapp, it must be easy to get a derogatory nickname. Gene Krapp's nickname was positive in nature, a tribute to his ability to handle a heavy workload. A righty who did his best work for Buffalo in the Federal League, Krapp's lifetime record was 38-47, but his ERA was a respectable 3.23.

Hands **Chuck Cottier** 2B, 1959-69

Cottier was a good-field, no-hit second baseman for several major league clubs in the 1950s and '60s. He *must* have been a good fielder, because he hung around for nine years despite a .220 lifetime average.

Iron Hands **Chuck Hiller** 2B, 1961-68

Hiller was the opposite of Chuck Cottier, a bad-fielding second sacker whose bat was his main asset. Hiller was the second baseman on the Giants' pennant-winning 1962 club, hitting .276 but making 29 errors. Against the Yankees that year, Hiller became the first

National League player ever to hit a grand slam in the World Series.

Three Finger **Mordecai Brown** P, 1903-16

As a child Brown lost one of his fingers and had another one badly mangled when he caught his hand in a threshing machine. The injury proved to be a blessing in disguise when he became a baseball player, because the gnarled hand helped Brown get a bigger break on his curveball. The ace of a great Cub pitching staff for many years, he had a lifetime winning percentage of .649 and a career ERA of 2.06.

Knuckles **Eddie Cicotte** P, 1905-20

Cicotte was finishing a 21-win season for the 1920 White Sox when it was revealed that he had conspired with several of his teammates to throw the 1919 World Series. He was immediately banned for life. His nickname suggests he was a knuckleballer, but there's some doubt as to whether Cicotte actually threw the pitch. His best pitch was the shineball, a pitch which behaved like a knuckler because Cicotte rubbed paraffin on the baseball.

Knucksie **Phil Niekro** P, 1964-87

Unlike Cicotte, Phil Niekro was definitely a knuckleballer. He used his best pitch to win 318 games, despite the fact that he usually was pitching for lousy teams. Like many knuckleballers, Niekro needed many years to perfect his money pitch, and his best years came when he was in his late 30s and early 40s.

Tom Thumb **Davy Force** 2B-SS, 1876-86

One of the game's early notables, Force was only 5-foot-4 and 130 pounds. He was named after the circus dwarf in the Buffalo Bill Wild West Show, Tom Thumb. Force was known as a slick fielder and lasted 10 years in the majors despite a .211 career average.

Bones **Steve Balboni** 1B, 1981-93

Also known as "Bye Bye" for his long home runs, Steve Balboni was anything but bony. The nickname is strictly a play on his last name. Balboni was a .229 lifetime hitter, but he belted 181 major league homers. Most of his best years came with the Royals.

Bone **Jay Buhner** OF, 1987-

Buhner's nickname is partly a play on his last name, partly a reference to his shaved head. After being traded away by the Yankees early in his career, he's become a cult figure in Seattle, with 268 home runs through 1998.

Limb **Frank McKenry** P, 1915-16

Skipper can find no documentation for how McKenry got his distinctive nickname, but at 6-foot-4 and 205 pounds, he was awfully large-limbed for someone pitching in the 1910s. He pitched only briefly in the majors (27 games), but his lifetime ERA was a respectable 3.10.

Babe Ruth's Legs **Sammy Byrd** OF, 1929-36

Another great nickname. Early in his career, Byrd's primary role was to serve as a pinch-runner and late-inning defensive replacement for the aging Babe Ruth. All those years as a scrub must have encouraged Byrd to pursue other means of making a living, and he did, becoming a successful professional golfer after leaving the majors at age 28.

Piano Legs **George Gore** OF, 1879-92

Though best-known for his distinctive nickname, Gore was a really good player, hitting .301 lifetime and leading the National League in walks three times. Despite the stocky legs that prompted his nickname, he once stole seven bases in one game.

Rubberlegs **Roscoe Miller** P, 1901-04

Miller got his nickname after jumping from the Tigers to the Giants in midseason 1902. His career was brief, but he won 23 games as a rookie for the 1901 Tigers. Years after his death, baseball archeologists unearthed the fact that he had led the NL in saves in 1903. . . with three.

Legs **Dick Weik** P, 1948-54

At 6-foot-3, Weik had very long legs, and that was the basis of his nickname. As a player, his most notable achievement was being traded even-up for two-time American League batting champion Mickey Vernon in June 1950. Considering Weik's lifetime record (6-22, 5.90), that has to rank as one of the worst trades in major league history.

Footsie **Clarence Blair** 2B, 1929-31

An infielder who played a few seasons with the Cubs, Blair got his nickname because of his speed afoot. As a player he is best known for taking over the Cubs' second-base job when Rogers Hornsby was injured in 1930. Blair was no Hornsby, and he lasted only one year as a regular.

Slewfoot **Cecil Butler** P, 1962-64

Butler was a big guy and very slow afoot. He pitched briefly for the Braves in the early 1960s; given the success he had (2-0, 3.31 in 11 games), it's surprising he didn't get more of a chance.

Turkey Foot **Frank Brower** OF-1B, 1920-24

Brower's daughter told Skipper that his nickname originally was Tuckey; some writers thought the name was Turkey, and called him Turkey Foot because of his speed. He didn't much like the name. Though he played in only 450 major league games, he was a good hitter: .286 lifetime with good peripheral stats.

Foots **Walker Cress** P, 1948-49

Cress was a big guy (6-foot-5) and a very slow runner. He pitched in 32 games for the Reds in the late '40s but failed to record a win or a save.

Deerfoot **Clyde Milan** OF, 1907-22

A good friend and Senators teammate of Walter Johnson, Milan was one of the fastest players of his generation. He won two American League stolen-base crowns, swiping 88 in 1912.

Corns **Hugh Bradley** 1B, 1910-15

Bradley suffered from corns on his feet but managed to steal 10 bases in 1915. That must have hurt his tootsies, because he promptly retired.

Bunions **Rollie Zeider** INF, 1910-18

Zeider played in the American League at the same time as Hugh Bradley, and one has to wonder whether they ever discussed their respective foot problems. The bunions didn't bother Zeider on the bases, as he stole 223 bases in the majors, including 49 as a rookie for the 1910 White Sox.

Dave Anderson's Favorite Nicknames

Babe **George Herman Ruth**

Yogi **Lawrence Peter Berra**

Dizzy **Jay Hanna Dean**

Shoeless Joe **Joe Jackson**

The Big Train **Walter Johnson**

Dave Anderson on baseball nicknames:

> "The best nicknames are those that become part of a player's name when people talk about him. . . such as Babe, Yogi, Dizzy, Shoeless Joe."

Dave Anderson writes the "Sport of the Times" column for *The New York Times*.

Thanks, Guys!

Somewhat less-than-complimentary nicknames given to players by their teammates and friends:

Nubby **Jesse Barnes** P, 1915-27

Barnes, who won 152 games for several National League clubs, was given this nickname by his New York Giant teammates. The reason? He had a very small head for a man who was six feet tall.

Squeaky **Ernie Bowman** INF, 1961-63

Utility infielder Bowman was dubbed Squeaky by San Francisco Giant teammates Willie Mays and Harvey Kuenn because he had a high-pitched voice. They were two of the biggest stars in baseball; Squeaky was a .190 hitter who got only 205 lifetime at-bats. Nobody ever said life, or baseball, was fair.

Stinky **Harry Davis** 1B, 1932-37

And you thought Ernie Bowman had it bad. The nickname, we're told, had nothing to do with a lack of cleanliness on Davis' part. It seems that there was a comic-strip character named Stinky Davis whom Harry was thought to resemble. His minor league teammates at Rochester thought so, anyway, and the name stuck.

Clinkers **Bill Fagan** P-OF, 1887-88

Fagan got his nickname because he was somewhat error-prone. His lifetime fielding percentage as a pitcher was .885. When they put him in the outfield for a couple of games, he had two putouts and three errors for a very nifty fielding percentage of .400. I'd say Clinkers was probably pretty accurate.

Stubby **Joe Erautt** C, 1950-51

Erautt was short and a little bit overweight as a child, so his friends in the little town of Vibank, Saskatchewan, christened him Stubby. Being stubby is no disadvantage when you're a catcher, and Erautt eventually made it to the major leagues with the 1950 White Sox. Unfortunately he couldn't hit (.186 lifetime), and a year later, it was back to the frozen tundra.

Midget **Don Ferrarese** P, 1955-62

Ferrarese—the name was pronounced Fur-ESS-eee—was only 5-foot-9, which is pretty short for a pitcher. I remember him mostly because I had his 1955 baseball card when I was a kid. I can still picture him in his Baltimore

---

Oriole uniform, grinning from ear to ear. A cute little guy. I was seven years old at the time; people thought I was a cute little guy, also. You could say that Ferrarese and I related to each other. I never would have *dreamed* of calling him Midget.

Nervous **Bob Friend** P, 1951-66

The ace of the Pirate pitching staff for several years in the 1950s and 1960s, Friend won an ERA title in 1955 and led the NL in victories in 1958. Despite his success, he always appeared to be acutely nervous prior to starting a game. He'd pace back and forth in the clubhouse, driving his teammates crazy.

Gumby **Jim Gantner** 2B, 1976-92

Gantner was nicknamed Gumby after the cartoon character, and there was something a little cartoonish about his personality. He was best known for his malapropisms, like "I was suffering from ambrosia."

Goofball **Billy Gardner** 2B, 1954-63

Like Jim Gantner, Billy Gardner was a middle infielder and one of the true characters of the game. Gardner had several different nicknames. He liked to refer to himself as Slick. Some people called him Shotgun because of his strong but erratic throwing arm. And at least a few of his teammates called him Goofball because of his odd but entertaining behavior. If Gardner minded, he never showed it.

El Divino Loco **Ruben Gomez** P, 1953-67

Gomez' nickname means "The Divine Crazy." He *was* a little crazy, and never really fulfilled the promise he showed as a second-year pitcher in 1954, when he went 17-9 for the World Champion Giants. He is best known for a beanball incident in 1956 involving Joe Adcock of the Braves. After getting beaned by Gomez, Adcock chased Gomez off the mound, around the field and all the way into the Giant dugout.

Floppy **Clint Hartung** P-OF, 1947-50

Baseball's most hyped rookie during the years just following World War II, Hartung turned out to be a colossal flop. The Giants never could decide whether to use him as a pitcher or an outfielder; as it turned out, he was nothing special at either spot. He

---

Thanks, Guys!   *151*

did have really big ears, which is where the nickname Floppy came from.

Pig **Frank House** C, 1950-61

Like Joe Erautt, Frank House was a catcher who was somewhat chubby when he was growing up in Bessemer, Ala. His friends nicknamed him Pig; you know, Pig House? Very funny. House had the last laugh; he signed a big bonus contract with the Tigers and went on to play 10 seasons in the major leagues.

Goofy **Mike LaCoss** P, 1978-91

LaCoss, who was a little bit flaky, was given the nickname Goofy by one of his San Francisco Giant coaches. He pitched in the majors for 14 years, but like Gomez, never really fulfilled the promise he showed in his second major league season (14-8 for the '79 Reds).

Twinkle Toes Bosco **Ron LeFlore** OF, 1974-82

Ron LeFlore was given this very unique nickname by a very unique group of individuals: his teammates on the prison baseball team while LeFlore was serving a sentence for armed robbery. Twinkle Toes was a salute to LeFlore's blazing speed; he also liked to put Bosco syrup in his milk, so they added that at the end. LeFlore eventually got out of prison and made it to the majors with the 1974 Tigers. He batted .288 and won two stolen-base crowns in his nine-year career.

Potato Head **Rudy Minarcin** P, 1955-57

Rudy Minarcin liked being called Potato Head! Or at least he wasn't embarrassed by it. Minarcin told Jim Skipper that the nickname listed for him in several other sources, Buster, was not correct. "My real nickname was Potato Head," he said. Minarcin told Skipper that when he was roughly nine years old, his father gave him a haircut; his friends thought the new 'do made Rudy look like Mr. Potato Head. So that became his nickname. And don't you forget it.

Rocky **Glenn Nelson** 1B, 1949-61

Nelson was christened Rocky by Cardinal teammate Enos Slaughter when he showed no reaction after a medicine ball bounced off his head. Nelson was a minor league star for many years, but never got an extended chance to show what he could do in the majors. He batted less than 1,400 times in nine major league seasons.

Line Drive **Lynn Nelson** P, 1930-40

Line Drive would have been a good nickname had Nelson been a hard-hitting outfielder. Unfortunately for him, he was a pitcher, and the nickname stemmed from all the line drives which opposing batters hit off him.

Bobo **Larry Osborne** 1B, 1957-63

Osborne got his nickname as a young minor leaguer with the Montgomery Grays. The teenager got a lot of attention from manager Charlie Metro, and Osborne's teammates concluded that he was Metro's "bobo," or pet player. Osborne had some power, but batted only .206 in six major league seasons.

Money Bags **Tom Qualters** P, 1953-58

Qualters was one of those 1950s bonus players who had to be kept on a major league roster for two seasons after signing. His Phillies teammates resented his healthy contract, and the nickname Money Bags was one indication of that. Qualters pitched only 34 games in the majors and never got a decision. But at least he had his bonus money.

Giz **Alex Sabo** C, 1936-37

Sabo told Skipper that this nickname, which is pronounced "Jiz," stemmed from the fact that he had trouble saying "Gee Whiz" when he was a child. So the neighborhood kids started calling him Giz, which is the way he pronounced the colloquialism. As befits the nickname, Giz had an abbreviated major league career, getting only eight at-bats, but he pounded out three hits for a nifty .375 lifetime average.

Grump **Bob Scheffing** C, 1941-51

Scheffing was playing golf with Cub teammate Charlie Root when Root missed a short putt on the 18th green to lose the match. Scheffing got on him pretty good, and Root responded by telling Scheffing he was a grump. From that day on, Grump was Scheffing's nickname. Scheffing wasn't much of a player (.263 lifetime), but he later became a major league manager for the Cubs and Tigers, winning 101 games (but no pennant) in 1961.

Weaser **Lou Scoffic** OF, 1936

Stop me if you heard this one before.
Kid has problems pronouncing something, gets a unique nickname as a result,
and goes on to have a short, but sweet, major
league career. Alex Sabo? No, we're talking about
Lou Scoffic now. Scoffic couldn't pronounce the word
"whistle" when he was a kid. It came out sounding like
"weaser," and Weaser became his nickname. His major
league stats were almost identical to Sabo's: seven at-bats,
three hits for the 1936 Cardinals.

Mortimer Snerd **Dick Selma** P, 1965-74

Mortimer Snerd was one of the dummies created by ven-
triloquist Edgar Bergen: a very likable character, but plenty
goofy and not too bright. That about sums up Dick Selma,
who was best known for leading cheers from the bullpen
for the Wrigley Field Bleacher Bums in 1969. Now *that's*
something you don't see in baseball any more.

Moonman **Mike Shannon** 3B-OF, 1962-70

Another real character, Shannon became a popular
broadcaster for the Cardinals after his career
ended. He's as colorful as an announcer as he was
as a player. I love it when Shannon says, "Old
Abner has. . . done it again" when he's announcing
an especially good game.

Smiley **Norm Siebern** 1B-OF, 1956-68

More ballplayer humor: the Yankees called Siebern smiley
because he never smiled at all. Ah, but he could play a little, making a couple of All-Star teams for the A's and leading the American League in on-base percentage in 1962.

The Nervous Greek **Lou Skizas** OF, 1956-59

Boy, those 1950s Yankees really worked on
building up the egos of their young players,
didn't they? Skizas, who came up around the
same time as Siebern, was called The Nervous
Greek because of the nervous mannerisms
he displayed prior to coming up to bat. Like a lot of failed
Yankee prospects, Skizas was eventually exiled to Kansas
City. He belted 18 homers in only 376 at-bats for the A's in
1957, then got traded to the Tigers, who mysteriously let
him rot on the bench. Who knows, maybe they thought he
looked too nervous to put in the lineup. Skizas got only 46
major league AB after that promising '57 season.

Pecky **Pete Suder** INF, 1941-55

Suder got the nickname Pecky from his grade-school class-mates, but he told Skipper he didn't know what the name meant. I don't know, either, but as a major leaguer Suder mostly pecked out singles, hitting .249 with 49 homers in 13 years.

Rocky **Ron Swoboda** OF, 1965-73

An early symbol of New York Met ineptitude, Swoboda hung around long enough to become one of the improbable stars of the Mets' championship season of 1969. Despite his Series heroics, he was known for making mental errors, and that's how he got the nickname Rocky.

Stumpy **Al Verdel** P, 1944

Verdel was only 5-foot-9 when he reached the major leagues, and even shorter during his sandlot days. His team-mates christened him Stubby. Like Sabo and Scoffic, Ver-del had a short but sweet major league career: his only appearance was for the Phillies on April 20, 1944, and he retired all three batters he faced.

Gummy **Joe Wall** C, 1901-02

One of the few lefthanded throwers to catch in the majors, Wall had a condition which forced his gums into promi-nence. Yet another guy with a brief but effective major league career, Wall batted .300 in 40 career at-bats.

Tommy Hutton's Favorite Nicknames

Lights **Elias Sosa**
"The lights were on, but nobody was home."

The Kid **Gary Carter**
"We're best of friends and I'll be calling him Kid when he's 75 years old."

Lefty **Steve Carlton**
"There have been many with the same nickname, but in my mind there's only one Lefty."

Rock **Tim Raines**
"We were never sure if it was for his body or his hands."

The Bull **Greg Luzinski**
"No explanation needed."

Tommy Hutton's favorite nickname story:

"Steve Rogers was known as Cy. We were never sure if it was for his Cy Young stuff or his sighs on the mound between pitches."

Former major league first baseman Tommy Hutton is in his third season of broadcasting Florida Marlins games.

Surprise!

Nicknames aren't always what they seem. A few examples:

Noisy **Grey Clarke** 3B, 1944

One of those guys who never shuts up? Not at all; Clarke spoke so infrequently that one of his minor league team-mates, Art Evers, decided to dub him Noisy.

Moose **Walt Dropo** 1B, 1949-61

Dropo, the American League Rookie of the Year in 1950, was a huge man at 6-foot-5 and 220 pounds. But his nickname sprang not from his size, but from the name of his hometown, Moosup, Conn.

Cocky **Ferris Fain** 1B, 1947-55

A two-time American League batting champion (1951-52), Ferris Fain did have a somewhat cocky personality. But his nickname was given to him by one of his teams' trainers, who thought Fain's eyes were cockeyed.

Gabby **Bill Henry** P, 1952-69

Like Grey Clarke, Bill Henry got his nickname because he was anything *but* gabby. But he silenced a few bats in his 16-year career as a major league reliever.

Skip **Gene Mauch** INF, 1944-57

Gene Mauch was a major league manager for 26 years, so Skip seems like a natural nickname for him. But Mauch was known as Skip from the time he was a small boy; his father gave the nickname to him, short for Skipper.

Bam **Brian McCall** OF, 1962-63

Was Brian McCall known as Bam because he was a hard-hitting slugger? No, he was known as Bam because his initials were B.A.M., for Brian Allen McCall.

Spike **Spike Owen** SS, 1983-95

The surprise here is that Spike wasn't a nickname at all—it was Owen's real first name. That's right, Spike Dee Owen. Did he have a couple of brothers named Glove and Bat?

Cap **Charles Peterson** OF, 1962-69

Captain of the team, a natural leader, maybe? No, Cap Peterson was just like Brian McCall: his nickname sprang from his initials. His full name was Charles Albert Peterson.

Styles **Chris Short** P, 1959-73

A fancy dresser, a guy who was always in style: Christopher Joseph Short, Esquire. Don't make me laugh. Short got his nickname because he was considered the worst-dressed player in baseball. His pitching, at least, was stylish. In the five-year period from 1964-68, Short won 17-plus games four times.

Moose **Bill Skowron** 1B, 1954-67

Bill Skowron was a pretty strong fellow, though hardly a moose at 5-foot-11 and 195 pounds. So where'd the Moose come from? Skowron was given his nickname by his grand-father, who thought young Bill's haircut made him look like Mussolini.

Muscles **Tom Upton** SS, 1950-52

If you're on to this game by now, you prob-ably figured out that Tom Upton hardly had any muscles at all. To say the least: Upton was 5-foot-11 and 160 pounds, and he managed only 11 ex-tra-base hits (two of them homers) in 525 lifetime at-bats.

Bud **Harry Weiser** OF, 1915-16

Harry "Bud" Weiser: the perfect Chris Berman nickname! In actuality, Weiser's middle name was Budson, and that's why people called him Bud.

Josh Lewin's Favorite Nicknames

Demando **Armando Benitez**
"A nickname hung on the petulant reliever by the Orioles' coaching staff. Armando was known for his unwillingness to 'go with the program.'"

Mickey **Jeff Manto**
"Only 500 homers shy of the other Mickey M."

Joe Table **Jose Mesa**
"Translated directly from the Spanish."

The Joker **Joe Randa**
"Randa's upturned mouth makes it appear as though he's always smiling."

The Big Hurt **Frank Thomas**
"Authoritative *and* poetic."

Josh Lewin broadcasts games for the Detroit Tigers and the Fox Network.

The Men in Blue

Great umpire nicknames:

Joe Doaks **Lee Ballanfant** NL, 1936-57

According to Larry Gerlach, Ballanfant got this nickname from one of his semipro managers. Why is a mystery, but it stuck.

The Singing Umpire **Bill Byron** NL, 1913-19

Byron, who was also known (of course) as Lord, used to make up rhymes and sing them to protesting ballplayers. Here's one, courtesy of Jim Skipper:

> "Let me tell you something, son
> Before you get much older,
> You cannot hit the ball, my friend
> With your bat upon your shoulder"

Wait'll Ken Kaiser hears about this.

King of the Umpires **John Gaffney** NL, 1884-1900

Gaffney was one of several 19th-century umps given this nickname. (A century later, there are a *lot* of umps who seem to think they're the king.) Gaffney must have been pretty good, given the way umps were abused during baseball's early days.

Easy **Tom Gorman** NL, 1951-76

Gorman, an unpretentious sort, was given his nickname by the Phillies' high-strung infielder, Dick Allen. Quite a compliment, I'd say. Gorman, who wrote a book with the help of sportswriter Jerome Holtzman, had a knack for keeping control of a game without making a big fuss about it.

Bull-Necked Bill **Bill Guthrie** NL/AL, 1913-32

Bill Guthrie was definitely *not* easy; he was a rough, tough character who was not afraid to stand up to the rowdy players of his day. Skipper adds that he was a "dese/dem/dose" kind of guy who would say things like, "It's eeder dis or dat wit me. Dere ain't no in between."

God **Doug Harvey** NL, 1962-92

I'd say that this nickname was an even bigger compliment than "King of the Umpires." Universally liked and respected during his umpiring days, Harvey undoubtedly will be in the Hall of Fame sometime soon.

Dumplings **George Hildebrand** AL, 1912-34

Hildebrand was short and rather pudgy. One wonders how many players called him Dumplings to his face.

Honest John **John Kelly** NL/AA, 1882-97

What is this, Be Kind to Umpires Week? Kelly actually got his nickname long before he became an ump. Lee Allen relates that Kelly, who was stranded in a snowstorm, borrowed a horse and buggy from a farmer. He agreed to return the horse and rig the next day and pay the farmer two dollars. Kelly made it to his destination, but when he got up the next morning, he discovered that the horse had died. Kelly went back to the farmer, apologized profusely and offered to pay $20, a good price, to replace the dead horse. "From this day on, you're going to be known as Horse Killer Kelly," said the farmer. Well, not really, though that would have been a really cool nickname. What the grateful farmer actually said was, "You're honest, John Kelly," and *that* became Kelly's nickname.

Catfish **Bill Klem** NL, 1905-41

We now officially stop being nice to umpires. If you've ever seen a picture of Klem, who was probably the most famous umpire in major league history, you'd have to say that he really did resemble a catfish, especially those big lips and fishy eyes. Players and managers noticed this resemblance, and any time they wanted to make an early exit from the game, all they had to do was yell, "Hey, Catfish!" Klem was a National League umpire for 36 years, finally retiring at the age of 66.

King of the Umpires **Tom Lynch** NL, 1888-99

Back in our nice mode momentarily: another king. Lynch was so well-respected that he later became president of the National League.

Meathead **George Magerkurth** NL, 1929-47

Calling George Magerkurth "Meathead" produced the same result as hurling a "Catfish" at Bill Klem: the result was an immediate ejection. Magerkurth, who preferred to be called Mage, was an ex-boxer and a tough customer who was not afraid to mix it up with a player. There's a memorable picture of Magerkurth duking it out with Giant shortstop Bill Jurges in a 1939 contest;

Magerkurth wound up getting a 10-game suspension, as did Jurges.

Little Joe Chest **Bill McGowan** AL, 1925-54

McGowan, who was Ted Williams' favorite umpire, was considered the top ump in the American League during most of his career. He was a small, feisty man, and Little Joe Chest was a term of affection. McGowan was elected to the Hall of Fame in 1992.

King of the Umpires **Billy McLean** NL, 1876-84

Yet another king. . . actually the first king, as McLean was the first umpire to be given this nickname. McLean's umpiring career began with the beginning of Organized Baseball in 1871, and he was a charter ump when the National League began play in 1876. Like many of the early umpires, McLean was a rugged customer, and worked as a boxer during the winter months.

Silk **Francis O'Laughlin** AL, 1902-18

One of the first men to umpire in the American League, O'Laughlin got his nickname after he showed up at a wedding wearing a silk hat. "I never missed one in my life," O'Laughlin used to say, and he truly believed it.

Brick **Clarence Owens** NL/AL, 1908-37

It's said that Owens got his nickname when an irate fan threw a brick at him early in his minor league career. Typically, Owens didn't let that intimidate him. His motto was, "Call 'em fast and walk away tough."

Beans **John Reardon** NL, 1926-49

One of the more colorful umpires in National League history, Reardon was best known for his endless battles with Dodger and Giant manager Leo Durocher. He got his nickname when he was playing ball as a teenager. Reardon was at bat when a boisterous fan yelled, "Come on, Baked Beans, old boy, hit one!" From then on he was known as Beans.

Mayor Daley **John Rice** AL, 1955-73

Rice got his nickname because it was said that he bore an uncommon resemblance to the late Chicago mayor, Richard J. Daley. There was a pretty good overlap there: Daley's mayoral career began the same year that Rice became an American League umpire, 1955, and ended with his death in 1976, three years after Rice had put away his ball-and-strike indicator for good.

The Great Anticipator **Bill Stewart** NL, 1933-54

This nickname wasn't exactly a compliment: it was given to Stewart because he had a habit of making calls prematurely, which sometimes resulted in embarrassing mistakes. Stewart was probably best known for blowing a pickoff call at second base in the first game of the 1948 World Series between the Braves and Indians. Stewart called the Boston runner, Phil Masi, safe, although films later seemed to show he was out. Masi later came around to score the only run of the game, and Bob Feller lost to Johnny Sain, 1-0.

Honest Bill **Bill Summers** AL, 1933-59

Another longtime American League ump, Summers was known for being firm but fair. He wasn't nearly as famous as his AL contemporary, Bill McGowan, but many people considered Summers to be just as good an umpire.

Country Joe **Joe West** NL, 1976-

Also known as Cowboy Joe, West has made several country-and-western recordings. A number of National League players wish that he'd make a big hit record and be forced to quit umpiring. In a 1999 poll of NL players, West was voted one of the three worst umpires in the league.

Jim Callis' Favorite Nicknames

Death to Flying Things **Bob Ferguson**

Captain Hook **Sparky Anderson**

The Splendid Splinter **Ted Williams**

The Yankee Clipper **Joe DiMaggio**

Stan the Man Unusual **Don Stanhouse**

Jim Callis on nicknames:

> "The Splendid Splinter and The Yankee Clipper may be the two best nicknames ever. They capture the essence of the two best players of their generation."

Jim Callis is a Senior Editor at STATS, Inc.

Franchise
All-Nickname Teams

This section contains all-time nickname teams for 26 of the 30 major league franchises—all but the clubs from the two most recent expansions (1993 and 1998). No player could appear on more than one team, but the same person could appear as a player on one team and a manager on another. In picking the teams, I didn't just select the guys with the most interesting nicknames; I tried if possible to find *good* players who also had colorful or famous nicknames. I was looking for a combination of strength in nicknames and strength on the field, in other words. Sometimes the pickings were pretty slim, and some of the teams worked out a little better than others. But this is just for fun, and I think you'll enjoy looking over the teams. If you think you have better ideas about some of my selections, feel free to let me know.

Angels

MGR	Skip	Gene Mauch
C	Buck	Bob Rodgers
1B	Papa Jack	Ron Jackson
2B	The Iron Pony	Sandy Alomar
3B	Radio	Aurelio Rodriguez
SS	Little Duck	Dick Schofield
LF	Daddy Wags	Leon Wagner
CF	The Mighty Mite	Albie Pearson
RF	Mad Dog	Lee Thomas
SP	Dude	Rudy May
RP	The Hummer	Art Fowler

Most Enduring Nickname: Daddy Wags **Leon Wagner**
Most Colorful Nickname: The Growin' Samoan **Tony Solaita**

One of the best Angels nicknames—The Incredible Hulk, for Brian Downing—didn't make this list; Downing was primarily a DH, and when he played in the field, it was usually in left. Not even Downing could top Daddy Wags, Leon Wagner.

Browns/Orioles

MGR	Quaker	Johnny Oates
C	Scrap Iron	Clint Courtney
1B	Gorgeous George	George Sisler
2B	Ski	Oscar Melillo
3B	The Human Vacuum Cleaner	Brooks Robinson
SS	The Blade	Mark Belanger
LF	Bumble Bee	Al Bumbry
CF	Motor Mouth	Paul Blair
RF	Baby Doll	Bill Jacobson
SP	Crazy Horse	Mike Cuellar
RP	Stan the Man Unusual	Don Stanhouse

Most Enduring Nickname: Gorgeous George **George Sisler**
Most Colorful Nickname: Stan the Man Unusual **Don Stanhouse**

The St. Louis Browns were one of baseball's most inept franchises. Then they moved to Baltimore and found success. There are a few Brownies on this list, but most of the players come from the O's glory years.

Red Sox

MGR	Rough	Bill Carrigan
C	Pudge	Carlton Fisk
1B	The Hit Dog	Mo Vaughn
2B	Hobe	Albert Ferris
3B	Pinky	Mike Higgins
SS	Rooster	Rick Burleson
LF	The Splendid Splinter	Ted Williams
CF	The Gray Eagle	Tris Speaker
RF	Dewey	Dwight Evans
SP	Rocket	Roger Clemens
RP	The Monster	Dick Radatz

Most Enduring Nickname: The Splendid Splinter **Ted Williams**
Most Colorful Nickname: Dr. Strangeglove **Dick Stuart**

The Red Sox have been one of baseball's most consistently interesting franchises, and they've had more than their share of interesting nicknames. Surprisingly, some of their greatest players have *not* had nicknames: Bobby Doerr, Joe Cronin and Jim Rice, to name three.

White Sox

MGR	The Senor	Al Lopez
C	Cracker	Ray Schalk
1B	The Big Hurt	Frank Thomas
2B	Cocky	Eddie Collins
3B	The Ginger Kid	Buck Weaver
SS	Old Aches and Pains	Luke Appling
LF	Shoeless Joe	Joe Jackson
CF	The Bandit	Ken Berry
RF	Jungle Jim	Jim Rivera
SP	Black Jack	Jack McDowell
RP	Old Tilt	Hoyt Wilhelm

Most Enduring Nickname: Shoeless Joe **Joe Jackson**
Most Colorful Nickname: Old Aches and Pains **Luke Appling**

Great nicknames at every position. . . and no room for such great ones as Little Nel (Nellie Fox), Minnie (Orestes Minoso) or Jockey (Bibb Falk).

Indians

MGR	*Grover*	Mike Hargrove
C	*Honey*	John Romano
1B	*Tioga George*	George Burns
2B	*Bad News*	Odell Hale
3B	*Flip*	Al Rosen
SS	*Cotton*	Terry Turner
LF	*The Bedford Sheriff*	Elmer Flick
CF	*Rock*	Earl Averill
RF	*Stormy*	Roy Weatherly
SP	*Rapid Robert*	Bob Feller
RP	*Ears*	Don Mossi

Most Enduring Nickname: Rapid Robert **Bob Feller**
Most Colorful Nickname: Bad News **Odell Hale**

The Indians are currently going through the greatest period of sustained success in their history, but the only member of the current team represented here is the manager, Mike Hargrove. Manny Ramirez, Jim Thome, Kenny Lofton, Omar Vizquel—not a notable nickname among them. I find that surprising.

Tigers

MGR	*Ee-Yah*	Hughie Jennings
C	*Black Mike*	Mickey Cochrane
1B	*Hammerin' Hank*	Hank Greenberg
2B	*The Mechanical Man*	Charlie Gehringer
3B	*Freck*	Marv Owen
SS	*Donie*	Owen Bush
LF	*Slug*	Harry Heilmann
CF	*The Georgia Peach*	Ty Cobb
RF	*Wahoo Sam*	Sam Crawford
SP	*Prince Hal*	Hal Newhouser
RP	*Senor Smoke*	Aurelio Lopez

Most Enduring Nickname: The Georgia Peach **Ty Cobb**
Most Colorful Nickname: Fatty **Bob Fothergill**

A little weak on the left side of the infield, but what a great club otherwise. And what great nicknames. Check that outfield: three Hall of Famers, three great nicknames.

Royals

MGR	The White Rat	Whitey Herzog
C	Duke	John Wathan
1B	Bones	Steve Balboni
2B	Cookie	Octavio Rojas
3B	I-29	Bill Pecota
SS	The Flea	Freddie Patek
LF	Bo	Vince Jackson
CF	A.O.	Amos Otis
RF	Sweet Lou	Lou Piniella
SP	Flash	Tom Gordon
RP	Quiz	Dan Quisenberry

Most Enduring Nickname: The White Rat **Whitey Herzog**
Most Colorful Nickname: I-29 **Bill Pecota**

Considering all the success the Royals had from 1976 to 1985, their all-nickname team is surprisingly bland. The best nickname belongs to the manager, Whitey Herzog.

Senators/Twins

MGR	The Boy Wonder	Bucky Harris
C	Muddy	Harold Ruel
1B	Killer	Harmon Killebrew
2B	Buddy	Charles Myer
3B	The Walking Man	Eddie Yost
SS	Zorro	Zoilo Versalles
LF	Goose	Leon Goslin
CF	Deerfoot	Clyde Milan
RF	Bruno	Tom Brunansky
SP	The Big Train	Walter Johnson
RP	Firpo	Fred Marberry

Most Enduring Nickname: The Big Train **Walter Johnson**
Most Colorful Nickname: Abdul Jibber-Jabber **Lyman Bostock**

"First in War, First in Peace, Last in the American League." That's a famous description of the Washington Senators, and it's beginning to sound like the current-day Twins. A Senators/Twins All-Nickname team isn't bad at all, however—especially the starting pitcher.

Yankees

MGR	*The Old Perfessor*	Casey Stengel
C	*Yogi*	Larry Berra
1B	*The Iron Horse*	Lou Gehrig
2B	*Poosh 'Em Up*	Tony Lazzeri
3B	*Puff*	Graig Nettles
SS	*Crow*	Frank Crosetti
LF	*King Kong*	Charlie Keller
CF	*The Yankee Clipper*	Joe DiMaggio
RF	*Babe*	George Herman Ruth
SP	*Slick*	Ed Ford
RP	*Goose*	Rich Gossage

Most Enduring Nickname: Babe **George Herman Ruth**
Most Colorful Nickname: The Tabasco Kid **Norman Elberfeld**

The Yankee tradition is so great that you could easily pick a second team of great Yankees with great nicknames. How about an outfield of Long Bob (Bob Meusel), The Commerce Comet (Mickey Mantle) and Mr. October (Reggie Jackson), just for starters?

Athletics

MGR	*The Tall Tactician*	Connie Mack
C	*Blimp*	Frankie Hayes
1B	*Double-X*	Jimmie Foxx
2B	*Camera Eye*	Max Bishop
3B	*Home Run*	Frank Baker
SS	*Campy*	Bert Campaneris
LF	*Bucketfoot Al*	Al Simmons
CF	*Mule*	George Haas
RF	*Socks*	Ralph Seybold
SP	*Gettysburg Eddie*	Eddie Plank
RP	*The Eck*	Dennis Eckersley

Most Enduring Nickname: Home Run **Frank Baker**
Most Colorful Nickname: The Human Eyeball **Bris Lord**

The Athletics franchise has had its ups and downs, but the ups were extraordinary: dynasties in the teens, the late '20s-early '30s, the '70s and the late '80s-early '90s. These nicknames bring back memories of all the A's periods of glory.

Mariners

MGR	*Sweet Lou*	Lou Piniella
C	*Scrap Iron*	Bob Stinson
1B	*A.D.*	Alvin Davis
2B	*Juice*	Julio Cruz
3B	*Elvis*	Jim Presley
SS	*A-Rod*	Alex Rodriguez
LF	*Wimpy*	Tom Paciorek
CF	*Junior*	Ken Griffey Jr.
RF	*Bone*	Jay Buhner
SP	*The Big Unit*	Randy Johnson
RP	*Cuffs*	Bill Caudill

Most Enduring Nickname: Junior **Ken Griffey Jr.**
Most Colorful Nickname: Cuffs **Bill Caudill**

The Mariners have had some classic nicknames for a team that's only been around for a generation: Junior, A-Rod, The Big Unit. But they need nickname help at first base! Note to David Segui: do something outrageous.

Senators II/Rangers

MGR	*Popeye*	Don Zimmer
C	*Pudge*	Ivan Rodriguez
1B	*The Thrill*	Will Clark
2B	*Bump*	Elliott Wills
3B	*Toby*	Colbert Harrah
SS	*Scooter*	Scott Fletcher
LF	*The Capital Punisher*	Frank Howard
CF	*Gozzlehead*	Mickey Rivers
RF	*Igor*	Juan Gonzalez
SP	*The Ryan Express*	Nolan Ryan
RP	*Wild Thing*	Mitch Williams

Most Enduring Nickname: Pudge **Ivan Rodriguez**
Most Colorful Nickname: Emu **Jim Kern**

Nickname-wise, the Rangers are a little weak in the infield apart from first base, but the outfield is definitely first-rate. Pudge Rodriguez has taken Carlton Fisk's nickname and made it his own.

Blue Jays

MGR	*Cito*	Clarence Gaston
C	*Buck*	John Martinez
1B	*Big John*	John Mayberry
2B	*Little Hurt*	Craig Grebeck
3B	*Razor*	Rance Mullinicks
SS	*Gadget Man*	Tony Fernandez
LF	*Thrill*	Glenallen Hill
CF	*Devo*	Devon White
RF	*Shaker*	Lloyd Moseby
SP	*Boomer*	David Wells
RP	*The Terminator*	Tom Henke

Most Enduring Nickname: The Terminator **Tom Henke**
Most Colorful Nickname: Boomer **Greg Wells and David Wells**

For a team as successful as the Blue Jays, it's amazing how nickname-deprived they are. Thank goodness for John Cerutti, who sent me lesser-known nicknames. Still, a team that has both Boomer (Wells) and Shaker (Moseby) can't be all bad.

Braves

MGR	*The Miracle Man*	George Stallings
C	*The Senor*	Al Lopez
1B	*Goofy*	Joe Adcock
2B	*The Brat*	Eddie Stanky
3B	*Spike*	Clete Boyer
SS	*Rabbit*	Walter Maranville
LF	*The Roadrunner*	Ralph Garr
CF	*Jet*	Sam Jethroe
RF	*Hammerin' Hank*	Hank Aaron
SP	*Knucksie*	Phil Niekro
RP	*Bedrock*	Steve Bedrosian

Most Enduring Nickname: Hammerin' Hank **Hank Aaron**
Most Colorful Nickname: Glass Arm **Eddie Brown**

The Braves franchise has been around since 1876, but I had a surprisingly tough time filling out their all-nickname team. Clete Boyer, a *Yankee*, at third? Al Lopez, best known as the manager of the Indians and White Sox, behind the plate? Best I could do.

Cubs

MGR	*Jolly Cholly*	Charlie Grimm
C	*Gabby*	Charles Hartnett
1B	*Husk*	Frank Chance
2B	*The Crab*	Johnny Evers
3B	*Smiling Stan*	Stan Hack
SS	*Mr. Cub*	Ernie Banks
LF	*Old Hoss*	Riggs Stephenson
CF	*Hack*	Lewis Wilson
RF	*Swish*	Bill Nicholson
SP	*Three Finger*	Mordecai Brown
RP	*Everyday*	Don Elston

Most Enduring Nickname: Mr. Cub **Ernie Banks**
Most Colorful Nickname: Swish **Bill Nicholson**

The Cubs have as many great nicknames as any franchise in baseball. Unable to crack the starting outfield are such memorable names as Kiki (Hazen Cuyler), Circus Solly (Solly Hoffman), The Honker (Hank Sauer), Handy Andy (Pafko) and Zonk (Keith Moreland).

Reds

MGR	*Captain Hook*	Sparky Anderson
C	*Schnozz*	Ernie Lombardi
1B	*Doggie*	Tony Perez
2B	*Bid*	John McPhee
3B	*The Freshest Man on Earth*	Arlie Latham
SS	*The Boy Bandit*	Roy McMillan
LF	*Charlie Hustle*	Pete Rose
CF	*Bug*	James Holliday
RF	*Greasy*	Earle Neale
SP	*Eppa Jephtha*	Eppa Rixey
RP	*Professor*	Jim Brosnan

Most Enduring Nickname: Charlie Hustle **Pete Rose**
Most Colorful Nickname: The Freshest Man on Earth **Arlie Latham**

The Reds have a long history of colorful nicknames, beginning in the 19th century with The Apollo of the Box (Tony Mullane) and The Freshest Man on Earth (Alrlie Latham). You don't see nicknames like that any more!

Astros

MGR	*Flea*	Bob Lillis
C	*Skip*	Alfred Jutze
1B	*Bags*	Jeff Bagwell
2B	*Little Joe*	Joe Morgan
3B	*The Red Rooster*	Doug Rader
SS	*Sonny*	Roland Jackson
LF	*Cheo*	Jose Cruz
CF	*The Toy Cannon*	Jimmy Wynn
RF	*The Bull*	Bob Watson
SP	*Bee*	J.R. Richard
RP	*Fred Flintstone*	Fred Gladding

Most Enduring Nickname: The Toy Cannon **Jimmy Wynn**
Most Colorful Nickname: Fred Flintstone **Fred Gladding**

The Astros are a nice, clean, well-run franchise, but not very color-ful. You might call them "nickname-impaired." Skip, Sonny, Bags? I even had to recall Joe Morgan from the Reds' all-nickname team.

Dodgers

MGR	*Uncle Robbie*	Wilbert Robinson
C	*Campy*	Roy Campanella
1B	*Gentleman Jake*	Jake Daubert
2B	*Frenchy*	Jim LeFebvre
3B	*Penguin*	Ron Cey
SS	*Pee Wee*	Harold Reese
LF	*Babe*	Floyd Herman
CF	*Duke*	Ed Snider
RF	*The People's Cherce*	Dixie Walker
SP	*Dazzy*	Clarence Vance
RP	*The Vulture*	Phil Regan

Most Enduring Nickname: Duke **Ed Snider**
Most Colorful Nickname: The People's Cherce **Dixie Walker**

The Dodgers' colorful history is mirrored in their numerous color-ful nicknames. No room on this team for Ol' Stubblebeard (Bur-leigh Grimes), Skoonj (Carl Furillo) or Brickyard (Bill Kennedy), among others.

Pilots/Brewers

MGR	*Scrap Iron*	Phil Garner
C	*Simba*	Ted Simmons
1B	*Boomer*	George Scott
2B	*Gumby*	Jim Gantner
3B	*The Igniter*	Paul Molitor
SS	*Rockin' Robin*	Robin Yount
LF	*Spiderman*	Ben Oglivie
CF	*Stormin' Gorman*	Gorman Thomas
RF	*Tiny*	Mike Felder
SP	*Moose*	Brian Haas
RP	*Bigfoot*	Pete Ladd

Most Enduring Nickname: The Igniter **Paul Molitor**
Most Colorful Nickname: Mr. Warmth **Mike Caldwell**

The Brewers have been around for only 30 years, but they have a lot of great nicknames. And except for Tiny Felder, the starting lineup could kick a little butt, also.

Expos

MGR	*Buck*	Bob Rodgers
C	*The Kid*	Gary Carter
1B	*The Big Cat*	Andres Galarraga
2B	*Cool Breeze*	Rodney Scott
3B	*Coco*	Jose Laboy
SS	*Pepe*	Jesus Frias
LF	*Rock*	Tim Raines
CF	*Hawk*	Andre Dawson
RF	*Le Grande Orange*	Rusty Staub
SP	*El Presidente*	Dennis Martinez
RP	*The Terminator*	Jeff Reardon

Most Enduring Nickname: El Presidente **Dennis Martinez**
Most Colorful Nickname: Le Grande Orange **Rusty Staub**

As befits a team which plays in French-speaking Montreal, Expo nicknames are flamboyant, colorful and unusual. Their first hero was Le Grande Orange, Rusty Staub, their greatest pitcher El Presidente, Dennis Martinez. What a fun team this is.

Mets

MGR	*Bambi*	George Bamberger
C	*Mackey the Hacker*	Mackey Sasser
1B	*Mex*	Keith Hernandez
2B	*Hot Rod*	Rod Kanehl
3B	*HoJo*	Howard Johnson
SS	*Bud*	Derrel Harrelson
LF	*Mookie*	William Wilson
CF	*Nails*	Lenny Dykstra
RF	*Straw*	Darryl Strawberry
SP	*Tom Terrific*	Tom Seaver
RP	*Tug*	Frank McGraw

Most Enduring Nickname: Straw **Darryl Strawberry**
Most Colorful Nickname: Choo Choo **Clarence Coleman**

The Mets have had some years of glory and more than their share of colorful nicknames like Mookie (Wilson), Nails (Lenny Dykstra), Tug (McGraw), Dr. K (Dwight Gooden) and Choo Choo (Coleman). The players on this team can't compare with some of the others, but most of their nicknames are great.

Phillies

MGR	*Ace*	Jimmie Wilson
C	*Dutch*	Darren Daulton
1B	*Kitty*	Bill Bransfield
2B	*Kid*	Bill Gleason
3B	*Puddin' Head*	Willie Jones
SS	*Rowdy Richard*	Dick Bartell
LF	*The Bull*	Greg Luzinski
CF	*Slidin' Billy*	Billy Hamilton
RF	*Big Sam*	Sam Thompson
SP	*Old Pete*	Grover Cleveland Alexander
RP	*Turk*	Dick Farrell

Most Enduring Nickname: Old Pete **Grover Cleveland Alexander**
Most Colorful Nickname: Losing Pitcher **Hugh Mulcahy**

The Phillies have struggled throughout their history, and their all-nickname team isn't top-drawer, either. Only three Hall of Famers are on the team: Billy Hamilton, Sam Thompson and Pete Alexander.

Pirates

MGR	*The Hat*	Harry Walker
C	*Moon*	George Gibson
1B	*Eagle Eye*	Jake Beckley
2B	*Maz*	Bill Mazeroski
3B	*Pie*	Harold Traynor
SS	*The Flying Dutchman*	Honus Wagner
LF	*Pops*	Willie Stargell
CF	*Ginger*	Clarence Beaumont
RF	*Big Poison*	Paul Waner
SP	*Babe*	Charles Adams
RP	*Bones*	Kent Tekulve

Most Enduring Nickname: The Flying Dutchman **Honus Wagner**
Most Colorful Nickname: Kiki **Hazen Cuyler**

A Pirate all-nickname team would be a lot like the franchise's most successful teams: good overall offense but not many home runs; serviceable, but not great, pitching; and some great glove men. You can win with a team like that.

Cardinals

MGR	*Old Sarge*	Gabby Street
C	*El Gato*	Tony Pena
1B	*Sunny Jim*	Jim Bottomley
2B	*Rajah*	Rogers Hornsby
3B	*The Wild Horse of the Osage*	Pepper Martin
SS	*Slats*	Marty Marion
LF	*The Man*	Stan Musial
CF	*Hippity*	Johnny Hopp
RF	*Country*	Enos Slaughter
SP	*Dizzy*	Jay Hanna Dean
RP	*Cork*	Ted Wilks

Most Enduring Nickname: The Man **Stan Musial**
Most Colorful Nickname: Creepy **Frank Crespi**

The Cardinals have such a great nickname tradition that three of their players made the list of "Baseball's 25 Most Enduring Nicknames": Rogers Hornsby, Stan Musial and Dizzy Dean. If there was a spot for Greatest Baseball Executive Nicknames, you could add The Mahatma (Branch Rickey).

Padres

MGR	Trader Jack	Jack McKeon
C	Benny	Benito Santiago
1B	Crime Dog	Fred McGriff
2B	Bip	Leon Roberts
3B	Dirty Kurt	Kurt Bevacqua
SS	Jump Steady	Garry Templeton
LF	Mellow Carmelo	Carmelo Martinez
CF	Cito	Clarence Gaston
RF	Downtown	Ollie Brown
SP	Rain Man	Andy Benes
RP	Butch	Clarence Metzger

Most Enduring Nickname: Downtown **Ollie Brown**
Most Colorful Nickname: Jump Steady **Garry Templeton**

Downtown Brown is an all-time classic—but the Padres are a little thin at some positions. "Benny" was the best I could do for a Padre catcher, and this is probably the first time Dirty Kurt Bevacqua made the starting lineup on an all-Padre team.

Giants

MGR	The Little Napoleon	John McGraw
C	The Duke of Tralee	Roger Bresnahan
1B	Stretch	Willie McCovey
2B	The Fordham Flash	Frankie Frisch
3B	Peanut	Jim Davenport
SS	Beauty	Dave Bancroft
LF	Silent Mike	Mike Tiernan
CF	The Say Hey Kid	Willie Mays
RF	Master Melvin	Mel Ott
SP	Matty	Christy Mathewson
RP	Shooter	Rod Beck

Most Enduring Nickname: Matty **Christy Mathewson**
Most Colorful Nickname: Penitentiary Face **Jeffrey Leonard**

The Giants easily could have a Hall of Famer at every spot. Lindy (Fred Lindstrom) or Stonewall (Travis Jackson) could replace Jim Davenport at third; Pep (Ross Youngs) could replace Mike Tiernan; and Old Tilt (Hoyt Wilhelm) could replace Rod Beck.

John Dewan's Favorite Nicknames

No Neck **Walt Williams**

The Deacon **Warren Newson**

Little Hurt **Craig Grebeck**

Babe Ruth's Legs **Sammy Byrd**

Paw Paw **Charlie Maxwell**

John Dewan's favorite nickname story:

> "I feel fortunate to be a White Sox fan here in Chicago because Ken Harrelson, Chisox announcer, is single handedly keeping the art of nicknames alive. Big Hurt, The Deacon, One Dog, Little Hurt, Black Jack—all Harrelson specials.

> "Little Hurt is a nickname given to Craig Grebeck. It is a spinoff of Frank Thomas' Big Hurt. The idea was that Grebeck, in the eyes of Hawk and Wimpy (Tom Paciorek, Harrelson's sidekick) had a knack for putting 'a little hurt' on the ball, a la Frank Thomas. The irony is that, despite an occasional hurt on the ball, Grebeck is a utility infielder with little power as a hitter."

Lifelong White Sox fan John Dewan is CEO of STATS, Inc. and co-author of the annual *STATS Baseball Scoreboard*.

Bibliography

Ahrens, Art and Gold, Eddie. *Day by Day in Chicago Cubs History*. West Point, New York: Leisure Press, 1982.

Allen, Lee. *The American League Story*. New York: Hill and Wang, 1961.

------------. *The Cincinnati Reds*. New York: Putnam, 1948.

------------. *The Hot Stove League*. New York: Barnes, 1955.

------------. *The National League Story*. New York: Hill and Wang, 1961.

------------. *100 Years of Baseball*. New York: Bartholomew House, 1950.

Bouton, Jim. *Ball Four*. New York: The World Publishing Company, 1970.

Brosnan, Jim. *The Long Season*. New York: Harper & Brothers, 1960.

------------. *Pennant Race*. New York: Harper & Brothers, 1962.

Carter, Gary and John Hough Jr. *A Dream Season*. San Diego: Harcourt Brace Jovanovich, 1987.

Gerlach, Larry. *The Men in Blue: Conversations with Umpires*. New York: The Viking Press, 1980.

Hawkins, John C. *This Date in Baltimore Orioles & St. Louis Browns History*. New York: Stein and Day, 1982.

------------. *This Date in Detroit Tigers History*. New York: Stein and Day, 1981.

Hunter, Jim and Armen Keteyian. *Catfish*. New York: McGraw-Hill Book Company, 1988.

Lyle, Sparky and Peter Golenbock. *The Bronx Zoo*. New York: Dell, 1979.

O'Neill, Buck with Steve Wulf and David Conrads. *I Was Right on Time*. New York: Simon & Schuster, 1997.

Onigman, Marc. *This Date in Braves History*. New York: Stein and Day, 1982.

Riley, James A. *The Biographical Encyclopedia of the Negro Baseball Leagues*. New York: Carroll & Graf Publishers, Inc., 1994.

Ritter, Lawrence S. *The Glory of Their Times*. New York: The Macmillan Company, 1966.

Shatzkin, Mike. *The Ballplayers*. New York: Arbor House, 1990.

Skipper, James K. Jr. *Baseball Nicknames: A Dictionary of Origins and Meanings*. Jefferson, North Carolina: McFarland & Company, 1992.

Spink, J.G. Taylor and others. *Official Baseball Register*. St. Louis: The Sporting News, 1940-77

Stein, Fred and Nick Peters. *Giants Diary: A Century of Giants Baseball in New York and San Francisco*. Berkeley: North Atlantic Books, 1987.

Thomas, Henry W. *Walter Johnson: Baseball's Big Train*. Washington, D.C.: Phenom Press, 1995.

Walton, Ed. *This Date in Boston Red Sox History*. New York: Stein and Day, 1978.

Index

D

E

F

G

S

T

Index

About STATS, Inc.

STATS, Inc. is the nation's leading independent sports information and statistical analysis company, providing detailed sports services for a wide array of commercial clients.

As one of the fastest growing companies in sports, STATS provides the most up-to-the-minute sports information to professional teams, print and broadcast media, software developers and interactive service providers around the country. STATS was recently recognized as "One of Chicago's 100 most influential technology players" by *Crain's Chicago Business* and was one of 16 finalists for KPMG/Peat Marwick's Illinois High Tech Award. Some of our major clients are ESPN, the Associated Press, America Online, *The Sporting News*, Fox Sports, Electronic Arts, MSNBC, SONY and Topps. Much of the information we provide is available to the public via STATS On-Line. With a computer and a modem, you can follow action in the four major professional sports, as well as NCAA football and basketball. . . as it happens!

STATS Publishing, a division of STATS, Inc., produces 12 annual books, including the *Major League Handbook*, *The Scouting Notebook*, the *Pro Football Handbook*, the *Pro Basketball Handbook* and the *Hockey Handbook*. In 1998, we introduced two baseball encyclopedias, *The All-Time Major League Handbook* and *The All-Time Baseball Sourcebook*. Together they combine for over 5,000 pages of baseball history. We also published *Ballpark Sourcebook: Diamond Diagrams*, an authoritative look at major and minor league ballparks of today and yesterday. In addition to the new title you're holding, the *Football Scoreboard* kicks off its inaugural season. These publications deliver STATS' expertise to fans, scouts, general managers and media around the country.

In addition, STATS offers the most innovative—and fun—fantasy sports games around, from *Bill James Fantasy Baseball* and *Bill James Classic Baseball* to *STATS Fantasy Football* and *STATS Fantasy Hoops*. Check out our immensely popular Fantasy Portfolios and our great new web-based product, STATS Fantasy Advantage.

Information technology has grown by leaps and bounds in the last decade, and STATS will continue to be at the forefront as both a vendor and supplier of the most up-to-date, in-depth sports information available. For those of you on the information superhighway, you can always catch STATS in our area on America Online or at our Internet site.

For more information on our products, or on joining our reporter network, contact us on:

America Online — (Keyword: STATS)
Internet — www.stats.com
Toll Free in the USA at 1-800-63-STATS (1-800-637-8287)
Outside the USA at 1-847-676-3383

Or write to:

STATS, Inc.
8130 Lehigh Ave.
Morton Grove, IL 60053